Christian Humanism
and the Reformation

Christian Humanism
and the Reformation

Selected Writings of Erasmus

with the Life of Erasmus by Beatus Rhenanus

Edited by
JOHN C. OLIN

Revised Edition

New York
Fordham University Press

LC 65–10218
ISBN 0–8232–0987–3 (*clothbound*)
ISBN 0–8232–0988–1 (*paperback*)

First edition, Harper Torchbook, 1965
Reprinted by arrangement with
Harper & Row, Publishers, Inc.

Second edition, revised, 1975
second printing, paperback, 1976

Printed in the United States of America

JOHN MANIATTY

τῷ φίλῳ τῷ ἀληθεῖ

Abbreviations

Allen—*Opus epistolarum Des. Erasmi Roterodami.* Edd. P. S. Allen, H. M.
   Allen, and H. W. Garrod. 12 vols. Oxford, 1906–1958.
Nichols—*The Epistles of Erasmus.* Trans. and ed. Francis Morgan Nichols.
   3 vols. London, 1901–1918.

Contents

Illustrations

Foreword

Whatever their reactions to his books and opinions, contemporaries of Erasmus generally agreed on his celebrity and influence. Professor Olin reminds us of Dean Colet's prediction in 1516: "The name of Erasmus will never perish." Johannes Eck, remembered now for his opposition to Luther, criticized Erasmus as well but acknowledged in 1518 that "Except for a handful of monks and paltry theologues, nearly all men of learning are Erasmians." Although the fracture of Christendom a few years later involved Erasmus in bitter and prolonged controversies, his achievements as the author of the *Adages*, *Praise of Folly*, and *Colloquies*, as classical scholar, Biblical editor and commentator, and writer on religious and moral topics brought him fame which endured long after the sixteenth century. He remained a familiar name among scholars as long as Latin was the international language and the basis of literary culture. That era is gone, yet Erasmus is still known and read, through translation, by students of literary, religious, and intellectual history. He has to be read, for in his thousands of letters and in his dialogues and essays he gives us vivid pictures of the European world of 1490–1536, together with wise and often witty comments on people and events, both secular and religious.

Despite his early popularity in England, where certain of his writings were soon translated, many of his important works were unavailable in English until quite recently, and some have not yet been translated. Sixteenth- or seventeenth-century English versions of the *Enchiridion*, *Praise of Folly*, and some of the *Colloquies*, selections from the *Adages* and a few of the moral and educational works, or copies of his *Paraphrases* of the New Testament could be found in old editions or reprints. Bailey's version of the *Colloquies* (1725) was several times reprinted in the nineteenth century; early in the twentieth century *Ciceronianus*, some of the educational treatises, and three volumes of the letters became available. The Latin texts were to be found, as a rule, only in the older or larger academic libraries. If those libraries had copies of the Leiden edition of *Erasmi opera omnia* (1703–06), well and good, but not all of them had it. P. S. Allen's splendid edition of Erasmus' correspondence began to come out in 1906 and was completed in 1958, but was of little use to those unskilled in Latin and Greek.

The situation has improved remarkably in the last thirty years. More reprints of older translations have appeared, and many of Erasmus' major works, or generous selections from them, have been translated. The Leiden *Opera omnia* was reprinted in facsimile in 1961–62. A new, critical edition of the *Opera omnia*, the work of many scholars, is now in progress (vol. 1, 1969). This, the Amsterdam edition, will be the standard text of Erasmus' writings. Meanwhile another enterprise, for which readers of Erasmus in English must be grateful, has been launched from Toronto: the *Collected Works of Erasmus* (vol. 1, 1974), which will contain English versions of all of Erasmus' major works.

In part this extraordinary activity in editing, translating, and studying Erasmus so evident in the last generation may have owed something to the observance in 1936 of the quatercentenary of his death, an occasion which called forth many reassessments. Probably it owes much to the temper of Vatican Council II (1962–65). The deep and continuing interest in ecumenism among Christians in recent years has been accompanied by renewed and extended interest in Erasmus as a theologian. To some degree this emphasis on his theological, devotional, and Biblical labors was a proper reaction against older views of him as mainly a moralist or, at best, as a precursor of nineteenth-century liberal theologians. However that may be, it has illuminated Erasmus' place in sixteenth-century Christianity.

Nevertheless certain Erasmian texts of unusual value for anyone curious about his career and attracted to his religious thought, particularly his response to the Lutheran movement, remained virtually inaccessible to English readers until publication of the present volume in 1965. The *Compendium Vitae* had been printed only once in English, in F. M. Nichols' unfinished translation of Erasmus' letters, now out of print. Even though the authenticity of the *Compendium Vitae* is still debated, it is a document deserving attention, and to have it here with the biography of Erasmus by Beatus Rhenanus, his friend and favorite editor, is an advantage. Erasmus' letter to Dorp (1515) defending his *Praise of Folly* was never available in English at all. Nor, so far as I know, was the *Axiomata*. Portions of *Paraclesis*, a very important statement of what is commonly called Erasmus' Christian humanism, were quoted frequently, but the full text had not been printed in English translation since Erasmus' lifetime. The letter to Abbot Volz introducing *Enchiridion militis christiani* is one of the best expositions of Erasmian piety. The biographical sketches of Vitrier and Colet delineate the Christian life in two contemporaries Erasmus admired. Finally, in the letter addressed to Archbishop Albert of Mainz and the first letter to Jonas, we have incisive appraisals of the condition of the Catholic Church in the face of Luther's challenge.

Professor Olin's book provides reliable translations of crucial and characteristic expressions of Erasmian humanism. It was warmly welcomed as a useful collection when it appeared in 1965, and this new edition should prove equally useful to the growing number of Erasmus' readers.

University of Pennsylvania   CRAIG R. THOMPSON

Preface

I have made a few necessary corrections and have updated the bibliography in this second edition. I am happy to see these selections from Erasmus' writings once more in print, for the great humanist continues to speak, I believe, with particular relevance and meaning for us today. I am still indebted to those who helped me with the translation and preparation of the original edition, and I want to add my thanks now to Fordham University Press for making these selections again available.

Fordham University   JOHN C. OLIN

Christian Humanism
and the Reformation

Erasmus and Reform

Nomen Erasmi nunquam peribit : "The name of Erasmus will never perish." This imposing judgment passed in 1516 by the great English humanist John Colet may strike us as exaggerated today, for though Erasmus' name is still alive, the image evoked in most cases by his name is either that of the clever, irreverent author of *The Praise of Folly* or that of the fastidious and detached scholar suggested by Holbein's famous portrait in the Louvre. In both instances cleverness, sophistication, and the lack of serious commitment seem small grounds for immortality.

Perhaps Colet's judgment is too imposing, but at least it attests to the fame and importance of Erasmus in his own times. And his eminence among his contemporaries can be explained quite simply: he was the greatest scholar and writer of his age, and the significance of his scholarly achievement as well as the sincerity and integrity of his moral purpose were recognized by his whole generation. He had his enemies, to be sure, but the best and the mightiest acclaimed his worth.

So concise an explanation, however, does not exhaust the subject of Erasmus' ascendancy. There are still the questions of knowing what it was he achieved or sought to achieve, and of understanding the reason for the influence he exerted. And there may also be some confusion about the respect and authority he commanded in his day, for not long after Colet's prophetic declaration Erasmus was caught in the religious conflict in the sixteenth century that embroiled all of Christendom, and he became for many an object of suspicion and attack.

In a short essay, or indeed in a single book, all the questions that arise concerning Erasmus' influence and career cannot be answered, but it is the objective here, in view of the esteem in which his contemporaries held him, to explore a cardinal one. What was it that Erasmus did or tried to do? What was the fundamental purpose of his endeavors, the aim of his life's work?

This is a basic question because obviously all of Erasmus' thought and action hinge upon it. To know his underlying intention, to know the purpose that moved him, is to understand in large measure what he did and what he wrote and what the role was that he played in the Europe of his time. Such a question of course assumes a unity and constancy of purpose on the part of Erasmus, but that assumption shall be made at the outset and justified or not in the pages that follow. In fact a constancy of purpose along with a consistency in the ideas he expressed may even be said to be one of the most striking features of Erasmus' thought. His age was an age of change and cataclysm, but throughout the many years of his active life he remained extraordinarily true to the vocation and the ideal he had set for himself in his early days.

This question of Erasmus' aim or goal must first be approached against the background of his early life. The main facts, drawn from his *Compendium Vitae* (Selection I) and early correspondence, are clear enough. He was born in Rotterdam probably in the year 1466, and his birth was illegitimate. Raised by his mother, though his father, a priest, was apparently very solicitous about him and his education, he was sent to elementary school in Gouda and later to a famous school in Deventer staffed by the Brothers of the Common Life. His stay in Deventer warrants emphasis, for here in his truly formative years—from about 1475 to 1484—he made close contact with the *Devotio moderna,* that spirit and program of evangelical piety which characterized the work of the Brothers of the Common Life and which found its fullest expression in that great masterpiece of the spiritual life *The Imitation of Christ.* There he also gained an introduction to the new humanism or classical learning that was now making its appearance in northern Europe, for these years witnessed the expansion of that enthusiasm for the literature of antiquity and that attempt to recover and restore it in its fullness which hitherto had been confined to the scholars of Italy. A noted humanist, Alexander Hegius, became headmaster of the school toward the close of Erasmus' stay, and the most celebrated German humanist of the day, Rudolph Agricola, delivered a lecture at the school which made a deep impression on the youthful mind of Erasmus.

His education at Deventer ended with his mother's death, soon followed by his father's, and Erasmus came under the care of guardians, who first packed him off to a dismal school at 's Hertogenbosch and then induced him to enter the monastery of the Augustinian canons at Steyn. This last step came to be the cause of much regret and bitterness for Erasmus, though at the time he appears to have adapted himself to the monastic life without great difficulty. He took his solemn vows after a year (that is, around 1488), he continued to cultivate his now lively interest in the Latin classics and the new humanist scholarship, and in 1492 he was ordained a priest. Not long after this he obtained an appointment as a secretary to the bishop of Cambrai, an important personage in the Low Countries at this time, and Erasmus left his monastery and the confines of his native

Holland to enter the wider world that now beckoned to his eager spirit.

He did not remain long in the service of the bishop of Cambrai. In 1495 he won his patron's consent to go to Paris, where he planned to study for his degree of doctor of theology. His experience at the University of Paris both appalled and repelled him. He saw nothing of value or virtue in the arid scholasticism to which he was exposed, and he became acutely aware of the contrast between the barren disputations of his present masters and the learning and eloquence of the ancients.[1] This aversion to the methods and practitioners of scholastic theology will find constant expression in the writings of Erasmus and is one of the keys to understanding his lifework.[2] However, all was not disappointment and pain in Paris, though it was on the whole a trying period of uncertainty and adjustment. He pursued his classical studies and entered the threshold of the Paris humanist circle. To support himself when aid from his bishop-patron proved inadequate, he tutored some well-to-do students in Latin literature and style. One of these was a young English noble, Lord Mountjoy, who invited Erasmus to visit England in the summer of 1499.

This visit, whose duration was about eight months, marks the turning point of his life. "He came there," writes Johan Huizinga, "as an erudite poet, the protégé of a nobleman of rank, on the road to closer contact with the great world which knew how to appreciate and reward literary merit. He left the country with the fervent desire in future to employ his gifts, in so far as circumstances would permit, in more serious tasks. This change was brought about by two new friends, whose personalities were far above those who

---

[1] See Erasmus' letter to Thomas Grey, August 1497. Allen, I, 190–97, and Nichols, I, 141–44.

[2] Denys Gorce, "La Patristique dans la Réforme d'Erasme," *Festgabe Joseph Lortz* (Baden-Baden, 1958), I, 233 ff, gives some interesting background relevant to late scholasticism and Erasmus' aversion to it.

had hitherto crossed his path: John Colet and Thomas More."[3]

Up to this time Erasmus was searching his way. Classical letters had more and more absorbed his interest, and this in turn had led to his departure from the monastery at Steyn and to his rejection of the scholasticism he encountered in Paris. His future, however, was not resolved, nor was his purpose clear. In England he found his bearings. There he met men whose learning tremendously impressed him and whose character and religious devotion he could respect. He saw, moreover, a union established between a humanist enlightenment and an authentic Christian purpose. In this the example and friendship of Colet were of the utmost importance. Colet was lecturing on the Epistles of St. Paul at Oxford at this time and was using the grammatical and historical methods of the humanists to blaze a new path in theological study.[4] In him the exciting possibilities of a humanism scriptural and Christian came alive, and Erasmus, child of the *Devotio moderna* that he was but revolted by the stagnant religious culture he had come to know, saw what his own task must be. Colet tried to persuade Erasmus to lecture on the Old Testament at Oxford, a companion work to his own lectures on the New; but Erasmus, conscious of his present inadequacy, refused the invitation. It is clear, nevertheless, that Erasmus then, or very soon afterwards, set the goal which would henceforth give direction to his life's work. This goal was, to put it succinctly, to employ humanism in the service of religion, that is, to apply the new scholarship to the study and understanding of Holy Scrip-

---

[3] J. Huizinga, *Erasmus of Rotterdam* (New York, 1952; Harper Torchbook edition, 1957, under the title *Erasmus and the Age of Reformation*), p. 29.

[4] On Colet and his influence on Erasmus, see E. H. Harbison, *The Christian Scholar in the Age of the Reformation* (New York, 1956), pp. 55 ff, and Frederic Seebohm, *The Oxford Reformers* (London, 1869). Erasmus' own biographical sketch of Colet is in the second letter to Jodocus Jonas (Selection IX).

ture and thereby to restore theology and revivify religious life.

Erasmus returned to Paris in early 1500, and then began that great career which continued with unusual dedication and singleness of mind down to his death in 1536 and carried him to a pinnacle of influence attained by few other writers or scholars in European history. It was a life of intense scholarly and literary activity, comparable, in his own view, to the labors of Hercules. It was a restless life, marked by frequent travel and change of residence. Paris, Louvain, Venice, Cambridge, Basel, Freiburg—all became his temporary home. His books and editions poured forth, his fame grew, he carried on an enormous correspondence with the great and learned of his day, he saw to his sorrow Europe torn by bitter religious argument, and he witnessed the early consequences of what he had come to call "the Lutheran tragedy."[5] But withal he remained faithful to the cause of Christian learning which Colet had inspired.

Shortly after his return to Paris in 1500 Erasmus published his first and one of his most popular works, the *Adagia*, a collection of eight hundred short excerpts and proverbs from the Latin classics for those who would increase their classical knowledge and improve their Latin style. But this kind of improvement was no longer Erasmus' primary concern. He was now engaged in the study of Greek, which he viewed as an essential preparation for the study of scripture, and conjointly he was absorbed in the correction and editing of the letters of St. Jerome, whom he had long cherished as a Christian scholar.[6] We have a most revealing letter from Erasmus to a close friend in Flanders at this time, in which he tells of his great design, his *magnum*

[5] This term, used frequently by Erasmus, is found as early as May 1521 in the preface written for his *Epistolae ad diversos*. Allen, IV, 499. The expression is also found in the *Compendium vitae* (Selection I).
[6] Allen, II, 210.

quiddam, "to restore the whole Jerome as great as it is, corrupted, mutilated, confused by the ignorance of the theologians," and he links this important project to the restoration of true theology, *vera theologia.*[7] It is clear that in his mind Greek and Jerome were the means toward reopening scripture itself and that on this kind of scholarship the true theology must be based.

In the fall of 1501 Erasmus interrupted these scholarly pursuits to write a moral treatise, a guide to Christian living which is of the greatest importance in understanding the orientation and development of his thought. In this treatise, *Enchiridion militis christiani* (*The Handbook of the Christian Soldier*), the gulf is bridged between the academic endeavors which now absorbed him and the reform of Christian life which became his constant concern. Scholarship, classical, scriptural, and patristic, was not to be an end in itself but was to conduct men to a better life. Learning was to lead to virtue, scholarship to God, and thus, as Erasmus saw it, the restoration of theology was to be the means toward the revival of a living and lived Christianity. It is here that we come to the core of "the Erasmian idea," to the essential meaning of that Christian humanism whose greatest apostle Erasmus was. And in the *Enchiridion,* written at the outset of his career, we have the program he will henceforth follow.

Erasmus composed the *Enchiridion* ostensibly for a soldier who he was afraid might fall among "the superstitious kind of religious" that would drive him into "a sort of Judaism, and teach him not to love but to fear."[8] Develop-

---

[7] Letter to James Batt, c. December 12, 1500. Allen, I, 325–29, and Huizinga, op. cit., pp. 200–2.

[8] Erasmus, *The Enchiridion,* trans. Ford Lewis Battles, in *Advocates of Reform from Wyclif to Erasmus,* ed. Matthew Spinka (London, 1953), p. 378. On the circumstances that prompted Erasmus to write the *Enchiridion,* see Allen, I, 19–20. The *Enchiridion* was first published in Antwerp in 1503. Froben in Basel brought out a new second edition in 1518, for which Erasmus wrote the letter to Volz (Selection V) as a preface.

ing the theme that life is a constant warfare against sin, he explains the weapons that the Christian must employ and the rules and precepts that must guide him in his unending struggle. Two fundamental and related ideas run throughout the book. One is that the great weapon of the Christian is the knowledge of Holy Scripture; the other is that religion consists primarily not of outward signs and devotions but of the inward love of God and neighbor. This latter idea is particularly emphasized—it will become Erasmus' master thought—and some of the most striking and characteristic passages of the *Enchiridion* express it:

You venerate saints; you are glad to touch their relics. But you contemn what good they have left, namely the example of a pure life. No worship of Mary is more gracious than if you imitate Mary's humility. No devotion to the saints is more acceptable and more proper than if you strive to express their virtue. You wish to deserve well of Peter and Paul? Imitate the faith of one, the charity of the other—and you will hereby do more than if you were to dash back and forth to Rome ten times. . . . And although an example of universal piety be sought most fittingly from Christ, yet if the worship of Christ in his saints delights you very much, imitate Christ in the saints, and to the honor of each one change one vice, or be zealous to embrace a particular virtue. If this happens, I will not disapprove those things which are now done in public.[9]

Or again:

Do not tell me therefore that charity consists in being frequently in church, in prostrating oneself before signs of the saints, in burning tapers, in repeating such and such a number of prayers. God has no need of this. Paul defines love as: to edify one's neighbor, to lead all to become members of the same body, to consider all one in Christ, to rejoice concerning a brother's good fortune in the Lord just as concerning your own, to heal his hurt just as your own.[10]

[9] Erasmus, *The Enchiridion*, pp. 337–38.
[10] Ibid., p. 345.

This of course is a rule—*the* rule—for the Christian life
which Erasmus draws from scripture, and he urges his
friend to the zealous study of the Word of God. He suggests that some of the pagan authors may be read as a pre-
liminary training, "for they are often good moral teachers,"
and he recommends the Platonists because "they approach
as closely as possible the prophetic and Gospel pattern."[11]
However, Holy Scripture "divinely inspired and perfected
by God its Author"[12] is pre-eminent, and there is never a
question in the *Enchiridion* (or any place else in Erasmus)
of reducing Christianity to a level with paganism or of
creating some kind of naturalistic religious synthesis. There
is sometimes a misunderstanding of Erasmus on this score,
but even a cursory reading of his works, it would seem, must
dispel it.[13]

In the interpretation of scripture he commends the ancient
Fathers—Origen, Ambrose, Jerome, Augustine—and he
warns against the modern theologians, those *neoterici,* who
drink in the letter of the Sacred Writings but not the spirit
or who rely on Duns Scotus and fail to read scripture
itself.[14] "Especially make yourself familiar with Paul," he
exhorts in his famous closing passage, wherein he also re-
veals that he has been working on a commentary on St. Paul
and for that purpose has studied ancient literature and
acquired a knowledge of Greek and Latin:

We have not undertaken their study for empty fame or childish
pleasure of mind, but long ago put our mind to it that we might with
exotic riches abundantly adorn the Lord's temple (which some persons
have too much dishonored out of their own ignorance and barbarous-

[11] Ibid., pp. 304–5.
[12] Ibid., p. 303.
[13] See Louis Bouyer, *Erasmus and His Times* (Westminster, Md., 1959),
pp. 161–64.
[14] Erasmus, *The Enchiridion,* pp. 305–6, 334.

ness). By these efforts the generous natural qualities can be kindled to the love of divine Scripture.[15]

One other feature stands out most forcefully in reading the *Enchiridion,* and that is Erasmus' emphasis on the mystical body of Christ. He is constantly calling his reader's attention to the fact that he is a brother to his neighbor, a member of the same body whose Head is Christ:

It is not the Christian's way to reason thus: "What have I to do with him? I know not whether he be white or black, he is unknown, he is a stranger, he never deserved anything well of me." . . . Consider this: he is your brother in the Lord, coheir with you in Christ, a member of the same body, redeemed by the same blood, a comrade in the common faith, called to the same grace and happiness in the future life.[16]

This concept, which Erasmus roots firmly in the great Pauline texts, inspires most of his moral injunctions and forms the basis of what we may call, for want of a better term, his social outlook. He is led thereby to denounce the selfishness, the indifference, the greed that contribute to the ills and injustices of the world:

Your brother needs your help, but you meanwhile mumble your little prayers to God, pretending not to see your brother's need.[17]

You gamble away a thousand pieces of gold in one night, while some poor girl, plunged into dire need, prostitutes her body and loses her soul, for which Christ poured out his soul. You say: "What has that to do with me? My own concerns take up all my thoughts." And afterwards will you see yourself a Christian with this mind, who may not even be a man? . . . The law punishes you if you take unto yourself what belongs to another. It does not punish you, if you take your possessions away from a needy brother. Yet even so Christ will punish you.[18]

[15] Ibid., p. 379.
[16] Ibid., pp. 358–59.
[17] Ibid., p. 320.
[18] Ibid., pp. 360–61.

He is also led to deplore disunity and dissension among Christians and its most terrible manifestation—war. It remains for his later writings to express more fully the social application of the scriptural message, particularly on the subject of dissension and war,[19] but there is no mistaking his realization of this application in the pages of the *Enchiridion*. In brief, Erasmus was already keenly aware of the relevance of Christianity to the problems of his day.

Erasmus thus emerges, as he begins those labors which thereafter will engage him, as a reformer—a reformer of theology, a reformer of morals, a reformer of society. The three spheres are intimately connected. The advance of humanist scholarship and the expansion of Christian knowledge are the means whereby the needed reforms will come. He is aware of the limitations of human learning, yet it is knowledge, not ignorance, that will reveal God's truth and God's way. His lifelong efforts are posited on that belief.

Practically the whole corpus of Erasmus' work can be interpreted in this light. Certainly the selections in this volume are consonant with these reform ideas, and a brief consideration of other important writings and editions of Erasmus will likewise bear this out and indicate as well both the later development of his reform program and the continuity of his thought. In this connection one cannot fail to speak of Erasmus' best known and most widely read book, *The Praise of Folly*. This little masterpiece, quite unlike anything else Erasmus ever wrote, was dashed off in 1509 at Thomas More's house in London, where Erasmus was recuperating after a long stay in Italy and an arduous journey back to England.[20] It is a book which lends itself to varying

[19] On the subject of war, see Erasmus' comments in the letter to Volz (Selection V) and his report of Colet's sermon in the second letter to Jonas (Selection IX).

[20] In the letter to Dorp (Selection III) Erasmus discusses the occasion for writing *The Praise of Folly* as well as the meaning and character of the book. It was first published in Paris in 1511.

interpretations, for it is a kind of seriocomic joke, expressing frequently the most outrageous things; yet, as its first English translator observed, in every sentence, "almost in every clause, is hidden, besides the mirth, some deeper sense and purpose."[21] This deeper sense and purpose, in perfect accord with the spirit of the *Enchiridion,* are simply to reveal the sham and hypocrisy of human affairs and to recall men to that higher folly of which St. Paul speaks, the folly of the Christian. Erasmus does this, however, not in the straightforward way of the moral teacher, as in the *Enchiridion,* although there are passages that are straightforward enough in *The Praise of Folly,* but with the wit, the irony, and the guile of a mischievous jester. The book therefore is subject to certain confusions and misunderstandings, and readers have frequently been shocked at what they consider the rejection of sanity or the mockery of sacred things. Actually, as Bouyer has pointed out, Erasmus "is simply laughing at humbug."[22]

Perhaps the most famous and remembered parts of *The Praise of Folly* are Erasmus' thrusts at religious superstitions and at the theologians, the monks, and the prelates who disfigure religion with their conceits and unchristian lives.[23] These occupy a fair portion of the book, and it is here that it has its most cutting effect. The theologians, as we might expect, are given some rough treatment. They are in the vanguard of the followers of Folly, who is personified in the book and who speaks throughout, and, wrapped in their syllogisms and self-pride, they are far removed from the spirit of the Gospels or Epistles, which moreover "they have no time to open."

---

[21] Sir Thomas Chaloner's introduction to his English translation, published in 1549, in E. M. Nugent, ed., *The Thought and Culture of the English Renaissance* (Cambridge, 1956), p. 59.

[22] Bouyer, op. cit., p. 100.

[23] Erasmus, *The Praise of Folly,* trans. Leonard F. Dean (Chicago, 1946), pp. 79–82, 95–104, 109–13.

Next to the theologians in happiness are those who commonly call
themselves "the religious" and "monks." Both are complete mis-
nomers, since most of them stay as far away from religion as possible,
and no people are seen more often in public. . . . They are so detested that it is considered bad luck if one crosses your path, and yet
they are highly pleased with themselves. They cannot read, and so
they consider it the height of piety to have no contact with literature.
. . . Most of them capitalize on their dirt and poverty by whining
for food from door to door. They push into inns, ships, and public
conveyances, to the great disadvantage of the regular beggars. These
smooth fellows simply explain that by their very filth, ignorance,
boorishness, and insolence they enact the lives of the apostles for us.
. . . They forget that Christ will condemn all of this and will call
for a reckoning of that which He has prescribed, namely, charity.[24]

These are strong words, but Erasmus, speaking through
the mouth of Folly, has reserved even stronger ones for unworthy popes. It is clear that he has in mind the pontiff then
reigning, Julius II, the warrior pope whom he had recently
seen in action in strife-torn Italy.

They fight for these things [i.e., the possessions of the Church] with
fire and sword, inflamed by Christian zeal, and not without shedding
Christian blood. They look upon themselves as true apostles, defending the bride of Christ, and scattering what they are pleased to call
her enemies. As if the church had more deadly enemies than impious
popes who by their silence cause Christ to be forgotten, who use His
laws to make money, who adulterate His word with forced interpretations, and who crucify Him with their corrupt life.[25]

This piercing thrust at the pope who was then at the helm
of the Church leads immediately into one of Erasmus' first
great condemnations of war—a pursuit which he rejected as
the very antithesis of the doctrine of Christ, who had called
us all to be one:

[24] Ibid., pp. 101-2.
[25] Ibid., p. 112.

War is so monstrous a thing that it befits beasts and not men, so violently insane that poets represent it as an evil visitation of the Furies, so pestilential that it causes a general corruption of character, so criminal that it is best waged by the worst men, and so impious that it has no relation with Christ. Nevertheless, our popes neglect everything else to devote themselves to war. . . . I can't decide [he humorously concludes] whether the German bishops taught the popes all this, or whether it was the other way around.[26]

The impact of *The Praise of Folly* was, and still is, considerable; but for its proper evaluation it must be read and understood in the light of certain facts. First, it is a particular and unusual kind of book, actually a fool's book—and fools, as Erasmus points out, can get away with murder.[27] Then the general context of its composition must be borne in mind. It was written in 1509 in a Europe still Catholic though desperately in need of religious reform.[28] Finally, Erasmus' deeper purpose must be grasped: this is, not simply to criticize the follies and evils of mankind but to amend a troubled world. Nowhere in *The Praise of Folly* does Erasmus actually attack the doctrines and institutions of the Church, but only those who, in his mind, have degraded and disfigured them. "Nor did I have any intentions in the *Folly*," he himself wrote to Dorp, "different from those in my other works, although the method may have differed."[29]

The year 1516 is a memorable one in the story of Erasmus. In that year Erasmus completed and published his

---

[26] Ibid., pp. 112–13.

[27] Ibid., p. 75. This point is also made in the letter to Dorp (Selection III).

[28] Erasmus is very conscious of this time element in the subsequent appraisal of what he had written. See Allen, IV, 499. He comments on this situation in the first letter to Jonas (Selection VIII), declaring that if he had foreseen what was coming, he would not have written certain things or he would have written them in a different way. Beatus Rhenanus in his life of Erasmus (Selection II) also reports that Erasmus often told him the same thing.

[29] The letter to Dorp (Selection III).

most widely heralded scholarly work, a Greek and Latin edition of the New Testament. That same year his publisher, John Froben of Basel, brought out his corrected edition of St. Jerome in nine volumes.[30] Both projects had been in preparation for many years, and their appearance may be said to mark the climax of Erasmus' career. His fame, his prestige, his influence now reached their height, and scholars everywhere acclaimed themselves *Erasmiani*— a term, by the way, which Erasmus reproved, for "we are all followers of Christ, and to His glory we all drudge, each for his part."[31] That same year he wrote his most important political treatise, *Institutio principis christiani* (*The Education of a Christian Prince*), dedicated to the young prince who would soon become Emperor Charles V, in which he counseled that "the teachings of Christ apply to no one more than to the prince."[32] And a few months later he wrote his great denunciation of war, *Querela pacis* (*The Complaint of Peace*), a remarkable document motivated by the most fervent Christian ideals but at the same time attuned to the circumstances and problems of his age.[33] It is hardly necessary to point out that in these works, as in his whole moral approach, Erasmus stands in striking contrast to another contemporary scholar and observer, Niccolò Machiavelli, whose own famous book *Il Principe* (*The Prince*) had been penned just a few years before. But if this contrast is exceedingly sharp, the similarity between the ideas of Erasmus and those expressed by Thomas More in *Utopia*, that supreme masterpiece of the Christian Renaissance, is very close. And 1516 is also the year of *Utopia*.

[30] On the background of this, see Beatus Rhenanus' life of Erasmus (Selection II).

[31] Huizinga, op. cit., pp. 98-99.

[32] Erasmus, *The Education of a Christian Prince,* trans. Lester K. Born (New York, 1936), p. 148. On Erasmus' political thought, see Pierre Mesnard, *L'Essor de la Philosophie Politique au XVIe Siècle* (Paris, 1936), chap. II.

[33] Erasmus, *The Complaint of Peace,* introd. William J. Hirten (New York, 1946).

1516 then was a year of achievement for Erasmus and his friends, and hope in the eventual triumph of their reform ideas ran high. Peace now reigned in Europe, new and promising young princes were at the helm in the great Christian states, and a new birth of learning seemed about to crown an era of universal concord. The golden age anticipated by the humanists, however, was not to be. In March 1517 Giovanni Francesco Pico della Mirandola at a closing session of the Lateran Council in Rome warned the assembled Fathers that if Pope Leo failed to heal the wounds of the Church like a good physician with lancet and lint, God himself would cleanse those wounds with fire and sword.[34] That terrifying prophecy soon came true. In the fall of 1517 Luther advanced to the center of the stage, and the high drama of religious revolt and disruption began. Erasmus henceforth was caught in the headlong rush of events, and his figure was overshadowed by the more vehement actors that now dominated the scene. He did not disappear into the wings. He remained active to the end, his authority still unrivalled in the learned world; but what he achieved or sought to achieve became now of lesser moment than the grave issues Luther raised. The hope, too, of the reform of Christian life and society within the traditional frame of Christendom, as Erasmus envisaged it, was soon dashed to the ground.

The relation of Erasmus to the Protestant Reformation, particularly to its causation—did he "lay the egg Luther hatched"?[35]—is a broad and somewhat equivocal question upon which the selections in this volume can unquestionably shed some light. There is an obvious connection between the biblical humanism represented by Erasmus and the theological approach of Luther. The two, however, should not

[34] Pierre Janelle, *The Catholic Reformation* (Milwaukee, 1949), p. 45.
[35] This is a contemporary charge attributed to the Franciscans of Cologne by Erasmus in a letter of December 1524. Allen, V, 609.

be identified, for it is just as obvious that Erasmus' understanding of scripture (and his attitude toward the Church) differed essentially from the convictions of the early Protestant leaders.[36] Nor should too great stress be laid on Erasmus' influence as a critic and a reformer in the causal background of Protestantism. Both Erasmian reform and Protestantism are symptomatic, so to speak, of many of the same conditions in the Church and in the religious life of the time. They respond to many of the same abuses, but their responses are basically divergent, despite some resemblance on certain points of criticism and on certain theological tendencies. The letter Erasmus wrote to Jodocus Jonas in May 1521 (Selection VIII) is very instructive in this regard. Erasmus opposed, both in their essence and in their effects, the "extreme remedies" which Luther now propounded.

It must also be acknowledged that Protestantism has a theological origin and doctrinal base quite distinct from Erasmian humanism. Therefore, to make Erasmus responsible in some way for Luther is to fail to do justice to both the unique role of Luther himself and Protestantism's own historic *raison d'être*. And it is to imply as well that Erasmus' cry for reform necessarily led to the disruption of the Church. There was indeed an historic nexus between reform and disruption in the sixteenth century, but that link will not be found in the thought and work of Erasmus.

It is true that in the beginning Erasmus had a certain

---

[36] The theological disagreement between Erasmus and Luther goes back as far as 1516. In October of that year Luther wrote Spalatin that he disagreed with Erasmus' understanding of St. Paul, a matter that was communicated to Erasmus by Spalatin in a letter in December. Allen, II, 415–18. And in March 1517 Luther wrote to his close friend John Lang: "My opinion of Erasmus decreases from day to day. . . . I fear that he does not promote the cause of Christ and God's grace sufficiently. For him human considerations have an absolute preponderance over divine." Quoted in Heinrich Boehmer, *Martin Luther: Road to Reformation* (New York, 1957), p. 160. See also Harbison, op. cit., pp. 105–6.

sympathy for Luther and felt that the source of his action, rash though in some respects he might deem it to be, lay in those evils and abuses in the life of the Church which he himself had so long criticized and condemned.[37] He saw, too, that many of Luther's critics and opponents were men whom he abhorred and who had in turn attacked his work, and he feared that their victory in the Lutheran quarrel would embolden them in their resistance to reform and enlightenment in general. But this initial approach must be examined carefully in its context, and one must especially bear in mind Erasmus' aim of working for reform within the framework of the Church. As the controversy involving Luther became more vehement and widespread, he indeed became alarmed about its eventual outcome. In late 1520 he observed with considerable prescience that "the case was tending toward a greater crisis than certain men suppose,"[38] and he began then to see it as taking on the proportions of a "tragedy," a great disaster. Yet he still sought to moderate the quarrel, to conciliate the factions, to prevent a serious breach within the Church—or at least this remained the bent of his mind and the natural direction of his efforts. He failed. And history seldom bestows its accolade on those who fail, but it is his endeavor that we seek to measure today.

By 1524 the time for compromise had passed, and Erasmus, pressed by many to write authoritatively against Luther, composed and published a significant work. This was his treatise *De libero arbitrio* (*On Free Will*), in which he rejected one of Luther's fundamental teachings in the name of Holy Scripture and man's own obligation to

[37] See the letter to Albert of Brandenburg (Selection VI). For an excellent review of Erasmus' relations with Luther and Lutheranism, see C. R. Thompson's introduction to his edition of Erasmus' *Inquisitio de fide* (New Haven, 1950).
[38] The *Axiomata* (Selection VII).

lead a moral life.[39] Upbraiding Luther for his intemperance
and excesses and for arguing so dogmatically against all the
Fathers, the councils, and the popes, he asserted a stand on
the difficult problem of free will and grace that is clearly in
the Catholic tradition. The debate that followed was sharp
and extensive, but Erasmus' primary concern nevertheless
remained the reform of Christian life and practice in the
Church, and he continued to work with all his energies toward that goal. "To refuse to remedy [the state of affairs
in the Church] in order the better to refute the Lutherans,
was, in his opinion, to cut the weed but leave its root,"
observes Bouyer.[40]

All through the 1520s he labored on new scholarly editions of the writings of the Fathers—Cyprian, Hilary,
Irenaeus, Ambrose, Augustine, John Chrysostom—and at
the time of his death in 1536 he was completing an edition
of Origen, his favorite among the Greeks. He also wrote
many moral and religious treatises—and in these years appeared numerous editions of his *Colloquies,* his most famous
book after *The Praise of Folly.*[41] In this work, which consists *in toto* of some fifty short dialogues or conversations,
we find much of the same wit and satire as in *The Praise of
Folly* together with those familiar and characteristic themes
he had expressed as early as 1501 in the *Enchiridion*: the
emphasis on Holy Scripture as the wellspring of Christian
piety, the need for a life of simple faith and charity as opposed to a life of external devotions alone, the rejection of
sham and pretentiousness in religious practice, the obligation to aid the poor, the revulsion at war.

[39] Erasmus–Luther, *Discourse on Free Will,* trans. E. F. Winter (New
York, 1961).

[40] Bouyer, op. cit., p. 192. See also Myron Gilmore, *Humanists and Jurists*
(Cambridge, Mass., 1963), Chap. V, for an excellent analysis of Erasmus'
position and attitude in his later years.

[41] *The Colloquies of Erasmus,* trans. C. R. Thompson (Chicago, 1965).

There is another theme prominent in the *Colloquies* which also deserves mention, namely, the way in which the Christian should face death. In "The Shipwreck" Erasmus tells the story of a ship caught and destroyed in a terrible storm. All on board are panic-stricken and in their distraught state scream to the saints for help and make extravagant vows. A young mother, with her child in her arms, alone retains her calm and dignity and prays in silence —and she is one of the very few who are saved. Again, in "The Religious Banquet," one of Erasmus' greatest colloquies, the attitude of Socrates in the face of death is discussed. His resignation and hope, so proper to the Christian, inspires Erasmus' interlocutor to utter these frequently quoted words: "I can hardly help exclaiming, 'Saint Socrates, pray for us.' "[42]

This theme may be an appropriate one on which to close this essay. As he tried to teach men how to live, so Erasmus also attempted to show them how to die. And he did this in the spirit that characterizes all his work—the spirit of evangelical simplicity which only the humblest and the wisest possess.The goal of Erasmus unquestionably was reform—the reform of theology through a return to scripture and the reform of Christian life and society as the consequence of a scriptural revival. But behind this broad purpose it is the return to the honesty and simplicity of the Gospels that is the ever dominant note. It is in this cause basically that the son of the *Devotio moderna* employed his learning and his humanism. And in this perspective the young Christian mother and the Socrates of the *Colloquies* become figures of considerable significance in grasping the purpose of Erasmus.

A French scholar, Gentian Hervet, who had studied in England and who served as a tutor in the Pole family, in 1526 translated into English a sermon of Erasmus, "On

---

[42] Ibid., p. 68.

the Mercy of God." In his preface to the sermon Hervet
has this to say in praise of his author:

He is the man to whom in learning no living man may himself compare. . . . He is the man that to Isaac may be compared, the which
digged up the goodly springing wells that the Philistines destroyed
and with dirt and dung overfilled. The clear springs of Holy Scripture that the Philistines had so troubled, so marred, and so defiled,
that no man could drink or have the true taste of the water, they be
now by his labor and diligence to their old pureness and clearness so
restored that no spot nor earthly filth in them remaineth.[43]

And it was for this reason that Colet had said that the name
of Erasmus would never perish.

[43] Nugent, op. cit., p. 349. This same kind of comparison to Isaac reopening
the wells which the Philistines had filled is used by Erasmus himself in the
letter to Volz (Selection V).

I

The *Compendium Vitae* of Erasmus of Rotterdam

The *Compendium Vitae* is a short autobiographical sketch composed by Erasmus in early 1524.[1] It was sent from Basel as a confidential memorandum to a very close friend, Conrad Goclenius, a professor of Latin at Louvain.[2] When Erasmus wrote this sketch, he was ill, depressed, and fearful of impending death, and he wanted to leave some sketch of his early years for the guidance of future biographers. He was entrusting these details about his private life to Goclenius, but he enjoined strict secrecy on him. This sketch (along with his letter to Grunnius in 1516 and a few other references) is the chief source for our knowledge of Erasmus' early life.

The *Compendium Vitae* apparently was not known until its publication by a Professor Paul Merula in Leyden in 1607. This circumstance, as well as the quality of the narrative, has caused its authenticity to be challenged. It is accepted, however, by the best authorities, and there seems little reason to doubt its genuine character.[3] Huizinga

---

[1] The Latin text is in Allen, I, 46–52. There is an English translation in Nichols, I, 5–13. The present translation was made by the editor from Allen with reference to Nichols' translation.

[2] Erasmus' covering letter to Goclenius is in Allen, V, 431–38. On Goclenius (1489–1539), see Allen, IV, 504–5. Erasmus' last surviving letter, of June 28, 1536, is addressed to him.

[3] Both Allen and Nichols accept it as genuine. See Allen, I, App. I, and Nichols, I, xlvii–li, 1–4. For a criticism of its authenticity, see Roland Crahay, "Recherches sur le *Compendium vitae* attribué à Erasme," *Humanisme et Renaissance*, VI (1939), 7–19, 135–53.

and other biographers have nevertheless questioned certain facts in the narrative, especially the "romantic" story of Erasmus' star-crossed parents.[4] This part of the account perhaps should be read with caution. Deeply sensitive to the illegitimacy of his birth, Erasmus in his later years may have depicted his origin and family background in somewhat imaginative terms. But even this is revealing, and it would be wrong to dismiss the memoir as a fabrication. It is a moving and extremely valuable document affording a unique insight into Erasmus' life and personality, and so great an Erasmian scholar as P. S. Allen judges its facts to be "correct even in small points."[5]

The narrative begins with short, jerky sentences, but it becomes more fluent, more like Erasmus' usual style as it progresses. The third person is used except at the very end when Erasmus speaks directly to Goclenius in the first person. These concluding remarks are not, strictly speaking, a part of the autobiographical sketch, and they should be read as a kind of postscript to it. The vigil of SS. Simon and Jude is October 27, and if the reference in the opening lines to his present age is understood exactly, the year of Erasmus' birth is 1466.

He was born in Rotterdam on the vigil of Simon and Jude. His age is about fifty-seven years. His mother was named Margaret, and the daughter of a certain physician Peter. She was from Zevenbergen. He saw two brothers of hers at Dordrecht, nearly ninety years of age. His father was named Gerard. The latter secretly had an affair with Margaret, in the expectation of marriage. And some say that they exchanged words of betrothal. The parents and brothers of Gerard were indignant about this. His father was Elias, his mother Catherine: both lived to a ripe old age, Catherine to nearly ninety-five. There were ten brothers, no sisters, of the same father and mother; all were married. Gerard was the youngest save one. It seemed to all that from so large a number one should be consecrated to God. You know the feelings of the old. And the brothers wished

[4] Huizinga, op. cit., p. 5, and Albert Hyma, *The Youth of Erasmus* (Ann Arbor, 1930), pp. 52 ff. Charles Reade's novel *The Cloister and the Hearth* is based on the story Erasmus gives of his parents and birth.

[5] Allen, I, 577-78.

to hold on to the property and to have a hospitable retreat for themselves. Gerard, seeing himself completely barred from marriage by the solid opposition of all, did what the desperate do; he secretly fled, and on his journey he sent his parents and brothers a letter inscribed with clasped hands and with the sentence, "Farewell, I shall never see you again."

Meanwhile, his intended wife was left with child. The boy was raised at his grandmother's. Gerard went to Rome. There he supported himself adequately as a scribe, for the art of printing was not yet in use. Moreover, he had a very fine hand. And he lived like a young man. He soon applied himself to liberal studies. He gained an excellent knowledge of Greek and Latin. And he even made unusual progress in the study of law. For Rome then bloomed marvelously with learned men. He heard Guarino. He copied all the authors with his own hand. When his parents learned that he was at Rome, they wrote him that the girl he had sought to marry was dead. Believing this, out of grief he became a priest, and he applied his whole mind to religion. When he returned home he discovered the deception. However, she never afterwards wished to marry, nor did he ever touch her again.

He provided a liberal education for the boy and sent him to elementary school when he was scarcely four years old. In his first years the boy made little progress in those disagreeable studies, for which he had no native aptitude. When he was in his ninth year, he was sent to Deventer; his mother followed to watch over and care for him in his tender age. That school was still barbarous (the *pater meus* was studied, tenses were required, Ebrardus and Johannes de Garlandia were read).[6] But Alexander Hegius

---

[6] The *pater meus* was probably a Latin declension exercise; Ebrardus was the author of an elementary Latin text; Johannes de Garlandia was a thirteenth-century poet studied in school.

and Zinthius had begun to introduce some better literature.[7] At last, from schoolmates who, being older, were in Zinthius' class, he first got the scent of better learning; later he heard Hegius several times, but only on feast days when he lectured to all. Here he reached the third class. Then a plague raging there carried off his mother, and the son, now in his thirteenth year, was left behind. When the plague daily became worse and worse and ravaged the whole house in which he lived, he returned to his home. Gerard, on receiving the sad news, became ill and died soon after. Both parents were not much more than forty years old when they died. Gerard appointed three guardians in whom he had the fullest confidence. The principal one was Peter Winckel, then a schoolmaster at Gouda. He left a modest legacy, if the guardians had administered it in good faith. And so the boy was sent away to 's Hertogenbosch, although he was ready enough for a university. In fact, they feared a university, for they had decided to rear the boy for the religious life.

He lived there—that is, he lost—nearly three years in the Brothers' House, as it is called, in which Romboldus then taught. This kind of man is now widely spread through the world, although the type is the ruin of good natural talent and the seedbed of monasticism. Romboldus, who was greatly attracted by the ability of the boy, began to urge him to join his flock. The boy pleaded the inexperience of youth. When the plague arose there, although he had been ill for a long time with a quartan fever, he returned to the guardians; and he possessed by this time a sufficiently fluent style developed from several good authors. One guardian had died of the plague; the other two, not having

---

[7] Alexander Hegius (1433–1498), German scholar and teacher, and one time student of Rudolph Agricola, became headmaster of the Deventer school in 1483, during Erasmus' last year there. John Zinthius (d. 1498) was one of the Brothers of the Common Life who taught at Deventer. See Beatus Rhenanus' reference to him in the next selection.

managed the legacy very well, began to promote a monastery. The young man, weak with a fever which had gripped
him for over a year, was not disinclined to piety; however,
he did shrink from a monastery. Therefore they gave him
time to consider. Meanwhile one of the guardians induced
others to entice, to threaten, to influence the unsteady mind.
And he had in the meantime found a place in a monastery of
canons, commonly called regulars, at a college near Delft
named Sion, the principal house of its chapter. When the
day came for the reply, the young man answered prudently:
he did not yet know what the world was, nor what the
monastery was, nor what he himself was; accordingly, it
seemed wiser that he should spend some years in the schools
until he knew himself better. When he saw the young man
firmly stating this, Peter immediately roared: "I have labored in vain then to prepare such a place for you through
many entreaties. You are a good-for-nothing, you have a
bad disposition. I give up my guardianship of you. Find
your own living." The young man replied that he accepted
the resignation and that he was old enough not to need
guardians. When Peter saw that he made no progress, he
induced his brother, who was himself a guardian, to conduct
the business. This one used flattery. Others seeking to influence the youth approached on every side. He had a companion who betrayed his friend.[8] And the fever pressed
upon him. Nevertheless, the monastery was not acceptable,
until quite by chance he visited a monastery of the same
order at Emmaus, or Steyn, near Gouda. There he found
Cornelius, who had been a roommate of his at Deventer.
He had not yet accepted the religious habit; he had seen
Italy, but he had returned without having learned much.
For reasons of his own he began to depict with marvelous
fluency the holy life, the abundance of books, the leisure, the

---

[8] Nichols, I, 9, explains this allusion as applying to Erasmus' older brother
Peter, who yielded to the guardians and entered a monastery.

peace, the angelic companionship. Why not? Childish affection drew him [Erasmus] toward his old companion. Some enticed him, some pushed him on. The fever weighed upon him. He chose this place, having no taste for the other. He was duped, however, until he took his religious habit. Meanwhile, although a young man, he sensed the absence of true piety there. Nevertheless, he encouraged the whole flock to study. Preparing to leave before his profession, he was restrained partly by human shame, partly by threats, partly by necessity.

He was professed. Finally, by chance he became known to the bishop of Cambrai, Henry of Bergen. The latter was hoping for a cardinal's hat, and he would have had it but for his lack of ready cash. For this journey he wished to have a man skilled in Latin. Thus, he [Erasmus] was summoned by him with the permission of the bishop of Utrecht, which by itself was sufficient. Nevertheless, he also secured the permission of the prior and the general. He joined the retinue of the bishop, retaining his habit, however. When the bishop lost all hope of a cardinal's hat, and he [Erasmus] perceived that the bishop was not very steadfast in his affection towards others, he arranged to go to Paris for the purpose of study. An annual stipend was promised; nothing was sent. Such is the way of princes. There at the college of Montaigu he took ill from the bad eggs and the unhealthy quarters, an illness in a hitherto most healthy constitution. And so he returned to the bishop. He was received honorably. He recovered from his illness at Bergen. He visited Holland with the thought in mind that he would remain with his brothers. But at their spontaneous urging he returned to Paris. There without the help of a Maecenas he lived rather than studied; and because of the plague which continued there for many years, he had to return each year to his own country. He shrank from the study of theology because he felt that his mind was not well disposed with the result that he might upset all of their fundamental principles and thereafter be branded a heretic. Finally, when the plague raged all the year, he was forced to move to Louvain.

Before that he had visited England at the invitation of Mountjoy, then his pupil, now his Maecenas, but more friendly than generous. At that time he won the good will of all worthy men in England, especially because, when he was robbed at the port of Dover,[9] he not only took no revenge for the injury but soon published a little book in praise of the king and of all England. Later he was called back to England from France by great promises, at which time he gained the friendship of the archbishop of Canterbury. When the promises did not materialize, he went to Italy, where he had always ardently longed to go. Now on in years, that is, about forty, he stayed a little more than a year in Bologna. Then he went to Venice and published the *Adagia*; after that to Padua, where he spent the winter; a short time later to Rome, where already a distinguished and favorable reputation had preceded him. Raphael, cardinal of St. George, especially was kind.[10] Great good fortune would not have failed him, except that he was called back to England at the death of Henry VII and the succession of Henry VIII by the letters of friends promising the richest rewards. There he had decided to spend the rest of his days; but when even then the promises were not fulfilled, he betook himself to Brabant, invited to the court of Charles, now emperor, to whom he was made a councilor through the efforts of Jean le Sauvage, the great chancellor.[11] The rest is known to you.

9 See Beatus Rhenanus' account of the Dover incident in the next selection.

10 This was Cardinal Riario, a nephew of former Pope Sixtus IV, and during the time of Erasmus' sojourn in Italy (1506–1509) one of the most prominent prelates in Rome.

11 Jean le Sauvage (1455–1518) was an important Netherlandish noble and a high official at the court of the youthful Charles V. He became chancellor of Burgundy in 1515 and chancellor of Castile in 1516.

He has given the reason for changing his attire in the first tract wherein he replied to the calumnies of Lee.[12] You yourself can describe his appearance. His health was always delicate; thus he was frequently beset by fever, especially during Lent because of the fish diet, the mere smell of which was offensive to him. His nature was straightforward; and he was so averse to lying that even as a child he hated boys who lied and as an old man even shuddered at the sight of such persons. Among his friends his language was rather free, sometimes too much so; and though often deceived, he could not, however, mistrust his friends. He was somewhat fastidious, nor did he ever write anything which pleased him. He was not even pleased with his own face, and it was only with effort that his friends forced him to agree to sit for a painting. He had lasting contempt for honors and wealth, nor did he hold anything before his leisure and freedom. He was an honest judge of the learning of others and would have been a unique patron of talent, if his means were adequate. In promoting scholarship no one accomplished more, and because of this he incurred the oppressive envy of the barbarians and monks. Up to his fiftieth year he had not attacked anyone, nor was he attacked by anyone's pen. He had determined to keep his pen altogether free from blood. Faber was the first to attack him, for Dorp's undertaking was checked.[13] He was always polite in his reply. The Lutheran tragedy had burdened him with unbearable ill will;

[12] Edward Lee was an English student at Louvain who in 1518 launched a sharp attack on Erasmus. Erasmus conducted bitter polemics with him for a number of years. The reference here is to Erasmus' abandoning his Augustinian canon's dress. See Beatus Rhenanus' explanation for this in the next selection. Lee later succeeded Wolsey as archbishop of York (1531-1544).

[13] Faber is Jacques Lefèvre d'Etaples (Faber Stapulensis), the famous French scholar, who took issue with one of Erasmus' annotations on the Epistle to the Hebrews in his 1516 edition of the New Testament. A controversy developed over this in 1517-1518. Martin Dorp, a Louvain theologian, criticized Erasmus' *Praise of Folly* and his projected New Testament in a letter of September 1514. Erasmus' reply to Dorp appears in this volume (Selection III).

he was torn apart by each faction, while he sought to serve the best interests of each.

I will enlarge the catalogue of my works;[14] from this also much may be obtained. Gerard Noviomagus has written me that some men are considering a life of Erasmus, part in verse, part in prose.[15] He himself desired to be provided with information privately, but I have not ventured to send it. If you happen to talk with him, you can share this with him. But it is not expedient to attempt anything with respect to a life unless circumstances themselves demand it. But about this perhaps at another time, or even when we meet.

When I had written this, Berckman came, burdened with lies.[16] I know how difficult it is to keep a secret; nevertheless I entrust everything to you alone. I have celebrated our Viandalus; Levinus will show you the little book.[17] Urge Ceratinus whenever he reads an author to take some notes.[18] Favor must be shown to Froben; I cannot always be with him. And on account of him I am burdened with great ill will. You know how craftsmen are. Again farewell.

[14] This is the Botzheim Catalogue (Allen, I, 1-46), first published by Froben in 1523 and greatly enlarged for a second edition in September 1524.

[15] Noviomagus is Gerard Geldenhauer (c. 1482-1542), who at this time was secretary to the bishop of Utrecht. He was a scholar and a close friend of Erasmus. He went over to Protestantism after 1525 and in his later years served as a professor at Marburg.

[16] Francis Berckman was a bookseller at Antwerp and a printers' agent. Through him in 1513 Erasmus arranged his first publication with the Froben press, a transaction discussed by Beatus Rhenanus in the next selection.

[17] Erasmus dedicated his *Paraphrasis in Tertium Psalmum* to Melchior Viandalus, a teacher at Tournai, in early 1524. Levinus was evidently the bearer of the letter and the *Compendium vitae* to Goclenius.

[18] Jacob Ceratinus, a scholar apparently at Louvain at this time, collaborated on a Greek lexicon which Froben published in the summer of 1524.

II

The Life of Erasmus
by Beatus Rhenanus

This short biography of Erasmus was written by a close friend and colleague, Beatus Rhenanus, in 1540.[1] It was commissioned by the Froben firm in Basel as a preface to the nine-volume edition of Erasmus' complete works which the famous printing house published in 1538–1540. It introduces volume I of this first authorized *Opera Omnia* and is in the form of a dedicatory letter to Emperor Charles V.

Beatus Rhenanus (1485–1547), the son of a butcher of Schlettstadt (Sélestat) in Alsace, was a noted scholar and editor in his own right. Along with James Wimpfeling (1450–1528), he was one of the most prominent members of the Strasbourg–Schlettstadt literary circle. He knew Erasmus very well and had worked for many years with him at the Froben press in Basel. His biography is the first extended account of the life of the great humanist, and as such it is a prime source for his life and the predecessor of all subsequent biographies of Erasmus. In writing this life Beatus enlarged an earlier sketch which he had composed in 1536, shortly after Erasmus' death, as a preface to Erasmus' last work, an edition of Origen.

Beatus' life is an interesting complement to the *Compendium Vitae*, and in several instances it elucidates references made in this latter work. It is particularly valuable on Erasmus' stay in Italy, about which not too much more is known, and on Erasmus' scholarly

---

[1] The Latin text is in Allen, I, 56–71. There is an English abridgment in Nichols, I, 25–37. The present translation was made by the editor from Allen with reference to Nichols' translation. On Beatus Rhenanus, see P. Adam, *L'Humanisme à Sélestat* (Sélestat, 1962), pp. 51–67.

labors. Beatus is speaking throughout as one who had long known and worked with Erasmus.

Erasmus was born in the early years of the reign of your great-grandfather Frederick III on the twenty-eighth of October at Rotterdam in Holland, your province in lower Germany, which the Batavi once held but which now is more famous to all students as the birthplace of one native son, Erasmus, than for the memory of its former inhabitants, however pre-eminent they were in feats of war. Because of this son Rotterdam will always boast and be esteemed by the learned. The next praise is claimed by Deventer, which undertook to educate the boy, who previously had been a chorister in Utrecht Cathedral, where, accustomed to take part in the musical presentations, he had served because of his small, high-pitched voice, after the fashion of cathedral churches. Alexander Hegius of Westphalia was then in charge of the school in Deventer, a man by no means deficient in scholarship and with some skill in Greek, which he acquired from Rudolph Agricola, whose close friendship he enjoyed after the latter returned from Italy, where he had attended the lectures of Guarino of Verona, teaching at Ferrara, and several other famous scholars. The talent of Erasmus soon shone forth, when immediately he grasped what was taught him and faithfully retained it, surpassing all his classmates. At that time there was among those who were called Brothers there—they were not monks, but lived and dressed like monks—John Zinthius, a man very well educated for that time; the grammatical commentaries which he published testify to this, and they brought him a great name in this period in the German schools. Delighted by the progress of Erasmus (for these long robed cenobites preside over certain classes of students and teach publicly), Zinthius on one occasion embraced the boy and said, "Well done, Erasmus, some day you will reach the very summit of learning," and he kissed and dismissed him. This prophecy was not mistaken, as all are aware. But deprived of both parents soon after this, Erasmus was thrust from the school of Deventer, a most fertile seedbed for every kind of monk, into a monastery of canons, called in addition regulars in the Latin term, by the evil design of a guardian who wished to be rid of his responsibility. There he had for several years as a companion in his studies William Herman, of Gouda, a youth most devoted to letters and the author of the *Odarum Sylva*. Aided and encouraged by this companion, there was no volume of the Latin authors he did not examine. By day and night, they engaged in study. The time which others of the same age slothfully wasted in jesting, sleep, and feasting, these two spent in perusing their books and exercising their pens.

Having heard of the fame of Erasmus, Henry, bishop of Cambrai and descendant of the princes of Bergen, invited the young man, now ordained a priest, to join him as he prepared to go to Italy and petition Rome [for a cardinal's hat]. For he saw that Erasmus had ability in letters and eloquence and that he was endowed with cultivated manners, as his gracefully written letters showed; and thus he could be useful as well as ornamental to his entourage if he had to transact business with the Roman pontiff or with the cardinals. It is not clear to me what prevented the bishop from undertaking this journey. William Herman was certainly much grieved that Erasmus had been taken from him, for thus he wrote in one of his odes:

> Now fate divides us,
> To you a boon, to me a bitter lot.
> Without me you go,
> Without me you gain the Rhineland glens, the Alpine peaks.
> Pleasant Italy will your happy haven be. Etc.

Although the bishop of Cambrai changed his mind about going to Rome, he nevertheless kept Erasmus at his court, delighted with his natural charm and with the distinction and candor of his youth. Here, truly amiable, he gained the friendship of many, especially of Antony, abbot of St. Bertin, who was of the same family of Bergen, and of James Batt, who was secretary to the council of the town of Bergen, to whom so many of his epistles are addressed and who later held a high position for a long time in the household of Anne of Borsselen, mother of Adolf, prince of Veere. Moreover, the bishop of Cambrai, considering the rich talent of his son Erasmus, willingly provided him with the means of going to Paris and of undertaking there the study of scholastic theology. He thus became a Scotist in the college of Montaigu; for among the theological disputants Duns Scotus was especially proclaimed because of his sharpness of intellect. And when he found the college life too hard, he gladly moved to the house of a certain English noble, who had two young English noblemen living with him; Mountjoy, I gather, was one of them. For the English saw that among the professors of literature in the entire university of Paris there was no one more learned or more faithful in teaching. For Faustus Andrelinus, otherwise intent upon writing his poems with great care, taught in a perfunctory way, seeking the applause of an ignorant audience by certain jokes more amusing than scholarly. Gaguin had been employed on missions to foreign princes and was not quite so accomplished in these studies, nor did he publicly teach.[2]

And from this time on Erasmus began to be known in England, which he himself visited shortly afterwards at the invitation of his pupils, who had returned home. After he

---

[2] Robert Gaguin (1433-1501) was a leading scholar and author in Paris. When Erasmus first arrived there in 1495, he made his acquaintance. Soon after this Erasmus wrote a commendatory letter to fill the blank space at the end of Gaguin's *De origine et gestis francorum compendium,* published in September 1495. This was Erasmus' first published writing. Thus his career, in a sense, begins with his association with Gaguin.

had stayed there a while, at the time of his departure he was deprived of nearly all his fortune by the customs collector at the port of Dover, and not yet aboard ship, he met shipwreck because he attempted to take out some gold pieces beyond the prescribed amount and without royal permission (Mountjoy and More, unaware of English law, persuaded him that there was danger only in the case of English money). This wrong, however, had to be endured in silence, for with the law opposing, there was no remedy. It did not, however, estrange the injured spirit of Erasmus, nor did it deter him from returning to England frequently afterwards. That region had then begun to abound in learned men: William Grocyn, Thomas Linacre, William Latimer, who had undertaken the study of literature in Italy and were renowned for their skill in both languages, and also John Colet, Thomas More, Richard Pace, and Cuthbert Tunstall, by all of whom he was eagerly loved. And as for the bishops, those who were more acquainted with literature did more for Erasmus and treated him more kindly. He taught for some time at the university of Cambridge; he also taught at Louvain, when he stayed with John Paludanus, the orator of that school. At last persuaded by friends, he traveled to Bologna with John and Bernard, the sons of Battista Boerio of Genoa, the physician of the English king; and he saw at length Italy, which he always had a great desire to see (this was not unmerited, because no place in all the world is more cultured in every way than this region). He accompanied them not as an attendant, for he had not undertaken the care of their conduct, nor as a teacher, but as one who would direct and supervise their studies, as his letter to Botzheim states. There, among the professors he gained the friendship of Paulus Bombasius, a learned man of stainless character, who in turn was greatly delighted with the genius and learning of Erasmus. For Beroaldus, the Achilles among professors of his time, had already died, and Baptista Pius, an unfortunate imitator of antiquity, dreamed of Oscans and Volscians. On the journey Erasmus, along with an English companion, was made a doctor of theology at Turin in the Cottian Alps. Thus he carried into Italy dignity and erudition, which others have been accustomed to bring back from that country.

While he completed at Bologna the volume of *Adagia* begun long before (for he had published at Paris many years previously a brief and rough specimen of his future work), he was forced by the following circumstance to change his monastic garb as a canon regular, which up to that time he had worn. There is a laudable practice in that city that if anyone is suspected of having the plague, a surgeon appointed for the purpose is summoned at once. In order that he can more easily be avoided by all who meet or pass him, because of the deadly infection, he is accustomed to wear a white napkin over one of his shoulders and to carry a rod in his hand. By chance one day Erasmus was walking alone through an unfrequented street in the town in his customary canon's dress. Two or three inexperienced youths met him there, and catching sight of his white scapular, they thought him to be the plague investigator; and as Erasmus proceeded along his way suspecting nothing, they threatened violence with stones they had gathered and pursued him with loud shouts, not, however, going beyond words. Surprised, Erasmus sought to know the reason for the indignation. Some people who had heard the brawling and were looking on from their houses told him that his scapular, tied in a knot at his side, had alarmed the youths, and that mistaken by the similarity in dress, they thought he was returning from some plague victim and had no intention of getting out of their way. Therefore, lest he incur a similar danger again, Erasmus sent a petition to Pope Julius II that he grant him permission either to wear or not wear his religious habit. Because of his singular merits this conces-

sion was made without difficulty, provided that he wear the
dress of a priest; and this Leo X for other good reasons,
not so much to lay down a rule of life as to show his esteem
of Erasmus, later confirmed in the fullest form (as they
say) : specially and expressly overruling each and every objection, and holding their contents to have been sufficiently
expressed and enumerated.[3] And who can doubt that the
Popes have full power in human constitutions of this kind,
when the interpreters of the law concede them no little
authority in the interpretation and regulation of matters
pertaining to divine law and the law of nations, and indeed
hand down that they have the power of freely disposing and
dispensing, to use their own phrase, except in articles of
faith?

When work on the *Adagia* was completed, he wrote to
Aldus Manutius to ask if he wished to undertake the printing of the book. The latter replied that he would do so
with pleasure. Erasmus then moved to Venice. When he
came to the printing shop, he was forced to wait a long
time before he was received because Aldus was busy correcting proofs and thought that he was one of those ordinary
visitors, who more out of curiosity than for the sake of
offering their help or counsel constantly descend on a man
busy with other affairs and are always annoying. When he
found out that it was Erasmus, he begged his forgiveness
and embraced him with great delight; and he received him
as his guest in the home of his father-in-law, Andrea Aso-
lani, the proprietor of that famed establishment, where he
shared a room with Jerome Aleander of Motta, renowned
for his knowledge of the three languages, now a cardinal.
Among others he also enjoyed the intimate friendship of the
noble Paulo Canale, of Ambrosio Nolano, an eminent physi-

---

[3] These lines quote and refer to Leo X's letter of January 26, 1517 (Allen,
II, 433-35), which dispensed Erasmus from wearing his canon's dress, permitted him to live in the world, and granted him the power to hold Church
benefices, despite the illegitimacy of his birth.

cian, and of Battista Egnazio. Nor was his stay in Venice a brief one, for he revised and published again two tragedies of Euripides, *Hecuba* and *Iphigenia in Aulis,* and he corrected the comedies of Terence and Plautus with special reference to their poetry. During that time Alexander, son of James, king of Scots, and already archbishop of St. Andrews in Scotland, was studying at Padua and attending the lectures of Raphael Reggio. Erasmus became his teacher of rhetoric, and he later moved with him to Siena. For he had sometime before parted with his Boerio pupils because of the ill-humor of their father, after spending a year with them. At Padua he was in the company of the most learned Marcus Musurus of Crete and Scipio Carteromachus of Pistoia, whose kindness I have often heard him extol. He had proof of their sincerity many times when he sought their advice while he was working on the corrupt manuscripts of such Greek authors as Pausanias, Eustathius, the interpreter of Lycophron, and commentaries on Euripides, Pindar, Sophocles, Theocritus, and similar authors, most of which were in the Aldine library. There was nothing so abstruse which Musurus could not explain, nor so involved which he could not disentangle: Musurus, truly the guardian and high priest of the Muses. He had read everything, he had weighed everything. He knew perfectly the forms of expression, the myths, the histories, the ancient rites. A remarkable dutifulness even enhanced this consummate erudition, for he had an aged Greek father whom he tended with loving and constant care. Scipio was endowed with a many-sided learning and with an upright character. Both died at Rome, Musurus having been made archbishop of Monovasia by Pope Leo.

While Erasmus lived in Siena in the house of the archbishop of St. Andrews, whom he taught and whose ability he often praised—the truth of his appraisal would have been more apparent if that most illustrious youth had not been killed shortly after, together with his royal father as he closed his flank in the battle in which the army of King Henry of England, whose sister was the wife of the king of Scots, clashed with the invading Scots, who were allied with the French[4] (Henry at that time being in Belgium and besieging Tournai at the instigation of Pope Julius II)— while there in Tuscany, I repeat, Erasmus obtained leave to visit nearby Rome. It is impossible to describe with what great applause and with what great joy he was received there among the cultured, not only among those of ordinary status but also among those resplendent in the rank of cardinal, especially Giovanni de' Medici, who chosen in the place of the dead Julius II took the name of Leo X, Domenico Grimani of Venice, and Egidio da Viterbo, most learned in the three languages, all distinguished men born and devoted to the encouragement of studies, in which they so uncommonly excelled. He also saw, as I recall hearing, that illustrious Thomas Phaedra, incomparably eloquent in extemporaneous speech, who evoked venerable antiquity by his recounting of plays and comedies. And he saw other professors. If he wished to remain in Rome, he was offered the office of a penitentiary, which would lead in the future to higher dignities; certainly the gain could not thereafter be considered of small account. But he had to return to the archbishop, with whom he afterwards went again to Rome, which that most noble youth wished to see before he returned to his native Scotland; and they visited not only Rome (though with the archbishop incognito, lest he trouble anyone) but Italy farther south as far as Cumae, and they stole into the cave of the sibyl, which is still exhibited by the natives there.

After the departure of the archbishop of St. Andrews, the memory of old friends whom he had left in England

---

[4] This is the battle of Flodden Field, September 9, 1513, in which James IV of Scotland and his son were killed.

prompted the hurried return of Erasmus to his homeland. And thus he traveled through the Rhaetian Alps first to Chur, then to Constance on the lake of Bregenz; and after he crossed the district of the Lentienses, who are at the beginning of the Martian forest, which in ancient times was Orcynium, he came through the Breisgau to Strasbourg, whence he was carried down the Rhine into Holland. Then, after greeting his friends at Antwerp and Louvain, he left for England. He was gripped by the longing to see the theologian John Colet, who was dean of St. Paul's in London, Grocyn, Latimer, Linacre, mentioned above, and especially Thomas More. His old Maecenas was William Warham, archbishop of Canterbury, primate of all England and chancellor of that realm, that is, the highest judge, who surpassed all the bishops of that island by his generosity. He gave him money and, in addition, the Aldington benefice in the diocese of Canterbury; and when Erasmus was hindered by a scruple from accepting this immediately because the whole income belonged rather to the pastor, who, at hand day and night, instructed the people under his care—that which no one can deny—the archbishop said to him hesitating, "Who lives more justly than you from an ecclesiastical income, the one who by your most useful writings instruct, teach, and help all the priests themselves who are in charge of the churches? and not only these, but also all the churches everywhere in the world, which they individually govern and serve." I well remember Erasmus more than once saying that princes have the duty of helping students by their own generosity; but that they, with the intention of sparing their own expense, took recourse in conferring priestly benefices, which the followers of learning are forced to accept so that they may be able to have the leisure for scholarship. He honored others, as, for example, Mountjoy with the dedication of the *Adagia,* and John Colet, the founder of a new school in London, with the twofold *De copia verborum et rerum,* to whom he once jokingly said that the publication of both *Copia* clearly made him a poor man. Thus he decided to make immortal his most distinguished Maecenas, William Warham, with the dedication especially of the works of Jerome.

Emulating Aldus, John Froben had printed quite handsomely the *Adagia* for eager students. Erasmus was moved by this pleasing edition and also by the renown of the more diligent firm, and since he knew that another, enlarged copy of the *Adagia,* formerly promised and intended for Badius,[5] together with several books of Plutarch recently translated, had gone astray to Basel in line with the plan of Francis Berckman, and that there all the works of St. Jerome were in the Froben press, he betook himself there also, pretending a journey to Rome in fulfillment of a vow. Nor had the report been groundless. For a long time ago John Amerbach, having completed the works of Ambrose and Augustine, had wholly devoted himself to the correction of the volumes of Jerome.[6] He had collected the old manuscripts from everywhere and had employed learned men to restore the Greek passages scattered throughout. One of these was John Reuchlin, the lawyer, who tried to fill in the empty gaps with the aid of dictionaries.[7] He was succeeded by a more successful corrector, John Kuno of Nuremberg, a Dominican who, having followed a better method, dili-

---

[5] Josse Badius, scholar and proprietor of the Ascencian Press in Paris, had printed a great many of Erasmus' works. On this episode, see Huizinga, op. cit., pp. 82–83.

[6] John Amerbach (c. 1430–1513) had founded the famous press in Basel which is generally associated with the name of his partner John Froben (c. 1460–1527). One of Amerbach's great ambitions was to publish good texts of the Doctors of the Church. His edition of Ambrose had appeared in 1492 and that of Augustine in 1506. The great edition of Jerome was brought to completion by Erasmus, who long had an interest in such a project, and it appeared in 1516, three years after Amerbach's death. On Erasmus and the Jerome edition, see Allen, II, 210–11.

[7] John Reuchlin (1455–1522) the famous German scholar and champion of the study of Hebrew literature, had law degrees from Orléans, Poitiers, and Tübingen. He was employed by Amerbach in this task in the summer of 1510.

gently replaced what had been either missing or corrupt from traces in the old documents. And this he could do as a man nearly more learned in Greek than in Latin, trained certainly in the best authors, and for several years one of the most attentive students of the best professors in Italy, Musurus and Scipio, whom we have mentioned above, and John of Crete. And now with Amerbach dead, his sons Bruno and Basil together with John Froben had begun the printing of Jerome and had advanced as far as the commentary on the Prophets. The elegance of the edition, and especially the extraordinary zeal and diligence of the Amerbach brothers in their correcting, pleased Erasmus, who as a new guest had been received immediately into the Froben house. Therefore if he himself was ever consulted when there was need for judgment because of variant readings in the manuscripts, he was there to help. But he particularly claimed the volumes of letters for himself and occupied himself in part in completing the marginal notes, which he had already begun a long time before, and in part in adding new annotations and arguments. This task was considerable. A greater one by far was added. Students in France and Germany separately desired an edition of the New Testament in Greek which they might add to the Old from Venice. Erasmus had formerly written annotations on it, following Lorenzo Valla.[8] When he found these among his papers, he hastily revised and enlarged them amid the din of the presses. Nor were they lacking who thought that the New Testament itself should be polished, having been written, or rather translated, it appeared, for the mass of Christians. And by virtue of his own willingness he complied with those

[8] Lorenzo Valla (1405-1457), the Italian humanist, had written *Annotationes* on the New Testament, which Erasmus discovered in a monastery near Louvain in 1504 and whose publication he arranged for by Badius in Paris in 1505. On Valla and Erasmus, see Harbison, op. cit., pp. 45-47, 84-87. On the background and publication of Erasmus' New Testament of 1516, see Allen, II, 164-66, 181-84.

advising this. In fact, he dedicated this work to Pope Leo X, who as the highest guardian of the same indeed deserved the dedication of the principal document of our religion. On the other hand he dedicated the revision of the works of Jerome to Archbishop Warham of Canterbury, a lasting monument of singular respect.

He returned then to lower Germany on account of business, and having come back to us a short time later, he went thither again at the time when Your Majesty was consecrated at Aachen with the symbols of the Roman Empire, whose antiquity [has been preserved] for us by the Goths themselves, Theodoric of Verona and others. Then he was at Cologne prior to the Diet of Worms, notable among those who were your councilors;[9] for you had most wisely taken him into this body a long time before, when Jean le Sauvage was still alive and held the post of great chancellor. After the meetings at Worms were over and the city of Tournai had been regained, when Your Majesty had again left Brabant for Spain, Erasmus returned to Basel intending to re-edit the *Adagiorum chiliades* and to complete the *Paraphrases* of St. Paul and the Gospels. It is doubtful whether he undertook these more because of the applause of students everywhere or whether he himself wrote them more out of the joy [in doing so]. "Here I am on my own field of action," he said. And so he was. He examined especially the old commentators, Ambrose, Jerome, Augustine, Hilary among the Latins, Chrysostom and his imitator Theophylactus among the Greeks. He himself merely adapted the style. One of these, namely the first Paraphrase on the Gospel of Matthew, he dedicated to Your Majesty, and the last he dedicated to your brother, King Ferdinand. Who, devoted to your court and bound by the most honor-

___

[9] It was at this time (November 1520) that Erasmus, in the train of Charles V, had the interview with Elector Frederick of Saxony, out of which came the *Axiomata*. See Selection VII.

able office, has honored you more greatly as a youth and as
the heir of so many kingdoms, who esteemed you more
when you were raised to the summit of the Roman Empire
by the unanimous vote of the princes? He prepared for you,
still a young man, the *Institutio principis christiani*, expressed in devout but short aphorisms, a little book (may
God so love me as this is true!) in which he who has been
destined for the administration of the highest affairs may
either himself learn the conduct worthy of a Christian as in
a mirror, or a teacher working with him may see with what
kind of first principles pertaining to a youthful education the
mind of rulers should be imbued while yet still tender. Indeed Erasmus has always sought by every kind of deference,
proper to a man of letters, to give honor to the most noble
House of Austria, cradle of so many Caesars, whose empire
is scarcely limited by the Julian and Rhaetian Alps and by
the northern ocean. The panegyric to your father Philip,
presented at the time of his return from Spain and regarded
by him with very great affection, demonstrates this; and
Philip deemed that this service should be followed by extraordinary munificence, first showing as if by some fortunate
omen, what great value the writings of this man would have
one day, and all but establishing a model which other great
men might emulate. Nor did it happen otherwise.

And indeed Erasmus knew a similar benevolence on the
part of many kings and popes, as yours in the first place,
august Emperor, as that of your brother Ferdinand, now
King, as that of King Henry VIII of England, by whom he
was addressed in letters from that prince's own hand when
his father Henry VII was still alive, and as that of Pope
Clement VII. Nor was Pope Adrian of another mind, if
Erasmus had wished to accept the benefice offered him or an
honorary post. Moreover, what might Erasmus not have
expected from Francis of Valois, king of France, if we consider his disposition and what he wished to bestow upon

him? He did not disdain to write in his own hand at the end of at least one letter that Erasmus' arrival would be most pleasing. That Pope Paul III, as much because of his opinion and inclination for Erasmian virtue and learning as for the result [it would have], was in fact prepared to favor him at every opportunity, this henceforth is clear because not only had the proposal been made that Erasmus be admitted into the college of cardinals, but the Pope himself also offered Erasmus the provostship at Deventer in the diocese of Utrecht, which is said to grant an income of six hundred gulden. He offered it, did I say? On the contrary, he bestowed it, not only dispatching an apostolic letter concerning it, lest the weariness and expense of the undertaking diminish the value of the benefice, but also in an affectionate letter addressing your sister Mary, the most illustrious queen of Hungary and your regent in Flanders, that in consideration of her filial devotion towards the Roman See and of her royal generosity towards deserving men, she take care that the occupancy of the afore-mentioned provostship be kept free from intruders for Erasmus. However, Erasmus, an autarch because he had determined to refuse a benefice, remained his own master, saying that he, who was about to die in a short time, had sufficient resources. Truly it would be a very lengthy affair to draw up a list of princes and bishops who were munificent to Erasmus.

Erasmus was not only honored by the princes, but also by the cities of Germany; and if he passed through them and the magistrates knew it, he was presented with wine, an honor shown to magnates and the ambassadors of cities according to the custom of the nation. This happened at Basel in my presence, at Constance on the lake of Bregenz, where the jurist and consul Bartholomew Blaurer of his own accord deigned to attend the banquet, at Schaffhausen under the auspices of the abbot and magistrate, at Freiburg-im-Breisgau, at Breisach, at Schlettstadt, at Strasbourg, and also at other places. For many had known that he was in the council of Your Majesty. Indeed, on account of the excellence of his learning, which was more clearly displayed in all his published books from day to day, he was deemed worthy besides that all should respectfully desire to honor him eagerly with the gifts they sent, none of which he sought, and to favor him with every kind of distinction. And if we commonly see those men who, if ever necessity demands, are prepared to defend their country at the peril of their lives distinguished by titles of military glory, how much more justly is he honored who of his own accord consumed, not any brief time, but his whole life in the service of letters, employing his talents to the public advantage, unmindful of his own enjoyment? He could have been great and daily have become greater at Your Majesty's court. Was not your former teacher, Adrian of Utrecht, raised to the highest pinnacle of ecclesiastical authority? He could have lived in splendor at the courts of whatever kings he wished; for who of the highest princes has not sought him? He could have dwelt in leisure and enjoyment, but he preferred the public usefulness of his studies to all honors and to the crass pleasures of this life.

It is probable that in addition to other motives the happy issue of a scholarly revival also greatly fired the man to pierce through no matter what. In Germany and France letters lay cold and lifeless; hardly anyone knew Latin, no one Greek. And behold, immediately when the *Adagiorum chiliades* and the *De copia verborum et rerum* were published, the knowledge of languages began to come forth, like the sun breaking through the clouds. Other books useful for this purpose appeared: Theodorus' *Grammaticae institutiones*, translated into Latin, and the texts in both languages of many Greek authors, fully suitable for those wishing to learn without the help of an instructor. For in this way even Hermolaus Barbarus, the immortal glory of Venice, is said formerly to have made progress in private study, by comparing versions of the most learned Gaza. And then, as if by a given signal, the best men were promoting the cause of letters in those countries. But the greatest aid of all was given by the Trilingual College established at the University of Louvain on the recommendation of Erasmus.[10] Jerome Busleiden, provost of Aire and brother of Francis, at one time archbishop of Besançon, who died while abroad in Spain, had left at his death great wealth; and as he had intended that this be used for students, Erasmus proposed to those who drew up the will that they found an athenaeum at Louvain where the three languages would be publicly taught by virtue of appointments to salaried posts. And from this institution, as if from a Trojan horse, innumerable men provided with a knowledge of languages have up to now come forth, and in turn they are going to hand this knowledge over to those favoring higher things. Your universal sway, mighty Caesar, has nothing more illustrious than this. This example also moved Francis, king of France, to give thought to the establishment of a similar college in Paris and by letter to summon Erasmus, on whose advice everything would be arranged. And he had already received a royal diploma for the security of the journey, but reasons intervened to prevent his departure. Nevertheless, professors were also appointed there. And so it is generally acknowledged that the growth of learning in these countries is due most of all to Erasmus. For what stone did he not move, as they say, that studies might advance? With what great openness did he hand over everything, wishing to be understood by all, although many explain obscure matters far more obscurely? When he was about to publish the *Adagia,* certain scholars said to him,

[10] There is an extensive history of this famous college in its early period: Henry de Vocht, *History of the Foundation and the Rise of the Collegium Trilingue Lovaniense, 1517–1550* (Louvain, 1951–1955), 4 vols.

"Erasmus, you are divulging our secrets." But he was desirous that these be accessible to all so that they might attain to complete scholarship. Because of this candor that scholar was abandoned who once said to Aldus Manutius in Venice as he was preparing to publish Greek commentaries on Euripides and Sophocles, "Take care in doing this lest the barbarians, aided by these studies, remain at home and fewer of them come to Italy." Now nothing was so insignificant that it did not engage this great man for the sake of students. He even deigned to correct and explain the song of Cato itself, together with its title, so that neither in great matters nor in small ones would his work be lacking. Indeed, anyone can hardly be mentioned who has done more for general studies.

France indeed has Budaeus, a prince of letters, with whom he is happily compared.[11] This scholar was not only the first to explain in a most learned and thorough fashion the very abstruse subject of ancient money, but he also analyzed most elegantly the ancient forms of speech of the jurists when he published his annotations on the Pandects, to the great glory of his nation (it cannot be denied); finally he composed commentaries on the Greek language, than which nothing more useful can be near the student of Greek. But our scholar has expended more labor on theological studies. And these studies he treated with somewhat greater freedom because he saw (I use his own words from a letter to a certain friend) too much deference being given to the prattler of theology, the old theology being utterly effaced and the theologians so absorbed in the subtleties of the Scotists that they do not approach the springs of divine

[11] Budaeus, or Guillaume Budé (1467-1540), was one of the greatest of the French classical scholars. There is considerable correspondence between him and Erasmus, some of it in Greek. Budaeus' very learned and extensive treatise on ancient coinage and its value, *De asse,* was published in Paris in 1515. His important work on the Pandects (the digest of Roman judicial opinions compiled for Justinian) had been published by Badius in 1508. He also published a Greek lexicon in 1529.

wisdom. Moreover, he saw that ecclesiastical discipline had declined far from the purity of the Gospels, that the Christian people were weighed down with many practices, and that the consciences of men were ensnared by various tricks. And on account of this state of affairs, he attacked the arrogance, the ambition, the greed, and the superstition of certain men wherever they may be with a rather free pen, flattering no one however powerful he may be, though today, however, many do this excessively. Nothing is more injurious to princes, especially ecclesiastical princes, as not pointing out clearly what they should do, while we praise what they do. In this regard he is never remiss. Although I do remember him often saying while he was alive that if he had foreseen such an age arising as ours, he would not have written many things or he would not have written them in the way he did.[12] But, thank God, we see some fruit from these admonitions. The body of theologians in his own time study Cyprian, Augustine, Ambrose, and Jerome in place of Alexander of Hales and Robert of Holcot.[13] Peter Lombard attempted to reduce diffuse theological study to a system in the collected books of the *Sentences,* as they are called. But his method is looked for in vain in the commentaries of modern authors. John of Damascus tried to do a similar thing among the Greeks. From the ancients one may learn of the most simple beginnings of the early Church, which little by little has grown to its present majesty. And without reading these authors, he who has been occupied only with the modern writers will discuss many topics injudiciously, [and he will have] a white rule, as

[12] Erasmus expresses the same thought in his letter to Jonas of May 10, 1521 (Selection VIII).

[13] Alexander of Hales is a thirteenth-century English Franciscan theologian, and Robert of Holcot is a fourteenth-century English Dominican theologian. The two men mentioned in the next sentences are Peter Lombard, a twelfth-century theologian whose chief work, the *Sentences,* was a basic theological text in the Middle Ages, and John of Damascus, an important eighth-century Greek theologian.

the proverb says, for measuring sacred things.[14] Therefore a knowledge of the ancient writers is very necessary for the future theologian; and it is to this knowledge that Erasmus has so greatly encouraged students, correcting their lucubrations and comparing them with the ancient models.

His books are extant, nor is it necessary to recount them by name. In a great number of passages he has added severe judgments, which as an outstanding quality and clear proof of the most resolute and discerning character I admire more than anything else. For I think that there has been no one for many generations now who has been more influential on judgment, a fact which is wont to affect the highest scholarship ultimately of all. To some, measuring everything severely by the structure and vocabulary of Cicero, it appeared that it was enough to be Ciceronian. But he himself always loved an open, extemporanous, pure, fluent, and lively style; and he made certain terms serve the Christian subjects which he treated. For he did not approve the superstition of those who restore certain empty ancient models rather than maxims that are concise and distinguished. Indeed, we admit that the age of Cicero was most pure and worthy of imitation, and that therefore it is a great felicity if anyone attains the genuine diction of that time during which the Latin language especially flourished. And we perceive that some men elegantly advance this cause, nor are we envious. But let them produce for our benefit as many useful, holy, and wise writings as the Christian world received from Erasmus, and we will agree with them and even praise the Ciceronians for piety and virtue.

He wrote a great part of these books at Basel in Froben's home situated on St. Peter's hill and part also at Freiburg-im-Breisgau. For he was forced to migrate with his baggage

---

[14] This apparently is a reference to the Lesbian measuring rule of soft lead (Aristotle, *Eth. Nic.* 5.10.7). In this context it would seem to mean no fixed principle or standard of judgment.

to that town, under the jurisdiction of your brother, King
Ferdinand, at the warning of Bernard à Gles, cardinal of
Trent, who feared lest anything happen to him at Basel
after the religious change took place. This change, however,
occurred far more peacefully than many foresaw because of
the prudence of the magistrates, and none of the clergy
suffered injury. At Freiburg he first lived in that magnificent
house which your grandfather Maximilian had formerly
ordered prepared for himself by Jacob Willinger of his
Majesty's treasury as a nest in his old age. Afterwards he
bought a house of his own. But when he was invited to
Brabant by your most illustrious sister Mary, queen of Hungary, whom you had made regent in the Low Countries at
the death of your aunt Margaret, and when his *Ecclesiastes*
was first about to be published, in order that he might be
present while it was going through the press and might add
the colophon to the work, as they say (for I do not know
what remained to bring it to a conclusion), and at the same
time in order that he might dispel the more tenacious ves-
tiges of illness by a change of sky, he sold his house and
returned after seven years to Basel with all his belongings,
the greatest part of which were books, staying as a most
welcome guest with his old friend Jerome Froben; and he
had this in mind, that when he had regained his health and
had completed those affairs which he had at hand, he would
go by ship down the Rhine to lower Germany. Meanwhile
arthritis, which for some time had been quiescent, again
seized the man and sorely distressed him so that he could
not be moved from the place, the change of sky having been
in vain. As the torments abated, he passed from a biped first
to a quadruped, then to a triped, supporting himself with
the help of crutches and gradually creeping forward. Whenever he unfolded one by one the letters which he had received in former years from various friends, on account of I
know not what new publication—and very many came into

his hands from those who had departed from this earthly scene—he repeatedly said, "And this one is dead"; and finally, "Nor do I wish to live any longer, if it please Christ the Lord." And so dysentery, the fatal misfortune, tormented him, feeble and destitute of strength though entirely sound of mind; and having gradually exhausted him, it at last brought his death with the greatest calm and acceptance as he implored Christ's mercy in his final, oft repeated words. He who, when he lived, treated the teaching of Christ with such sincerity, in death received without a doubt a full reward from the highest Judge.

Relying on the authority of your Majesty, he had made a will, in which he provided in a threefold way for the needs of the poor out of his resources left at the time of death, that is, for helping the ill and aged, for aiding virgins who lacked marriage dowries, and for assisting students. Boniface Amerbach, professor of law, having been designated heir, together with his associates executed the will in good faith according to the mind of the testator with regard to the payment of annual stipends and incomes, and he took care to do everything which Erasmus wished to be done with exactness. He himself placed on a pillar in the cathedral of Basel, adjacent to the tombstone bearing the sculptured device "Terminus," a memorial engraved in Siebengebirge marble to the excellent patron.

Your Majesty knew that in stature he was, as he himself describes More in one of his letters, neither tall nor noticeably short. His body was compact enough and well proportioned, but because it was of a very delicate constitution and was easily disturbed by even the least change, as, for example, in the matter of wine or food or air, it was subject in later years to frequent ills, including the stone, not to mention rheum, in itself the constant and common ailment of all students. He had a fair complexion, light blond hair in his youth, bluish gray eyes, a pleasant expression; his voice was thin, though his language was admirably straight-forward; his dress was dignified and grave, as befits an imperial councilor, theologian, and priest. He was most constant in retaining friendship, and whatever the cause, he never changed a dedication. He had a most excellent memory, for as a child he memorized all of Terence and Horace. He was generous to those in need, to whom, as elsewhere, he was always accustomed to give alms through a servant as he returned home from mass; but he was especially kind and generous to young students of promise and talent, if any should come to him in need of money for study abroad. In social intercourse he was courteous and pleasant, without a trace of arrogance, in every respect surely ἐράσμιος, that is, amiable; and he was sorry that he had not taken that name when he first began to write and to be known for his published books. "For who," he said, "has heard any mortal called Love?" That is what ἐρασμός means in Greek.

On the other hand, with regard to the publication in a single edition of the numerous books which he had written throughout his life, both sacred as well as secular, this most modest man at the time of his death made no provision, having been of the opinion that in the future these writings of his would certainly be disregarded by the more educated daily arising. But since the printers Jerome Froben and Nicholas Episcopius felt that students desired these writings brought together at the same time in that order which he himself, when alive, made known to John Botzheim and later to Hector Boece in the catalogue of his works,[15]—namely, first those which pertain either to literary instruction or to piety, then those of a moral character, then the *apologiae,* and in the last place the authors he

---

[15] Erasmus drew up a catalogue of his works in 1523 at the request of his friend, John Botzheim, canon of Constance. It was published by Froben and greatly enlarged for a second edition in 1524 (Allen, I, 1–46). He compiled another catalogue in 1530 for Hector Boece, principal of King's College, Aberdeen (Allen, VIII, 372–77).

had revised and completed—they resolved to gratify the students, and they undertook a project as magnificent as it is worthy of the approval of all. They were deterred neither by the magnitude of the expense nor by the greatness of the labor, whatever the final outcome might be, provided that they might complete the volumes of Erasmus' works, having followed principally the author's catalogue to Hector Boece as the more recent. They even added all of those by Amerbach, on which afterwards Erasmus also labored, having omitted, however, a tenth volume only by excluding other authors which he had revised. The same printers promise to bring out separately in the course of time also this work of his for students, if they will find a comparable audience. And this edition must be made not only for other reasons of importance but also because it protects the reputation of so great a master of letters, lest anyone, either with the intention of doing harm or with a desire for gain, seeking the favor that comes from the genius evidently Erasmian, constantly attribute to him something which he has not written (we know that this happened when he was alive), or which he has not acknowledged as his own, or which, though acknowledged, he thought scarcely worthy of publication.

Schlettstadt, June 1, 1540.

III

Letter to Martin Dorp

MAY 1515

This lengthy epistle is a defense by Erasmus of his *The Praise of Folly* and of the Greek and Latin edition of the New Testament which he was about to publish.[1] It is addressed to Martin Dorp, a professor of philosophy at the University of Louvain, who had written Erasmus in September 1514 criticizing his famous satire and his temerity in correcting the Vulgate text of Holy Scripture.[2] A controversy ensued, in which Dorp replied in August 1515 and Thomas More wrote a long letter to Dorp in Erasmus' behalf in October.[3] Chambers tells us that More "converted his antagonist."[4] At any rate, the attack was checked, as Erasmus states in the *Compendium Vitae,* and cordial relations continued between Erasmus and Dorp.

Dorp (1485–1525) was a scholar in the humanist tradition and an old friend of Erasmus. He had studied at the Collège du Lis in Louvain, and after completing his own course of studies in 1504, he taught philosophy there. He received a doctorate of theology in 1515

---

[1] The Latin text is in Allen, II, 90–114. The present translation was made from Allen by the Rev. John W. Bush, S.J., and Mr. Martin Feeney, S.J., and as far as the editor can discover, it is the first English translation of this important text to be published. *The Praise of Folly* was first published in 1511, and Erasmus' New Testament was brought out by Froben in February 1516.

[2] Dorp's letter of September 1514 is in Allen, II, 10–16.

[3] Dorp's second letter is in Allen, II, 126–136. More's letter to Dorp can be read in English translation in E. F. Rogers (ed.), *St. Thomas More: Selected Letters* (New Haven, 1961), pp. 8–64. There is a good account of the controversy in Henry de Vocht, *Monumenta Humanistica Lovaniensia: Texts and Studies about Louvain Humanists of the First Half of the XVIth Century* (Louvain, 1934), pp. 139 ff.

[4] R. W. Chambers, *Thomas More* (London, 1938), p. 253. See Allen's note (IV, 124–25) on Dorp's later attitude and relations with Erasmus.

and was subsequently admitted to the University's theological faculty —facts which cast some light, it would seem, on the nature and timing of Dorp's criticisms. Erasmus viewed Dorp's letter as inspired by others, that is, by certain Louvain theologians who were opposed to the new scholarship and who were using Dorp in this instance as their mouthpiece. Whatever the situation, the crisis passed. Dorp went on to become rector at Louvain in 1523, and long before that he had renewed his interest in and approval of humanist studies. When he died in 1525, Erasmus wrote his epitaph.

The letter to Dorp is perhaps Erasmus' most important apologia and is extremely valuable in understanding *The Praise of Folly* within the context of Erasmus' aims and lifework. It was also one of Erasmus' first letters to be published, appearing in a volume by Froben in August 1515. It was subsequently reprinted in early editions of *The Praise of Folly*. The version translated here is the printed version and is an enlargement of the letter actually sent to Dorp.

To MARTIN DORP, DISTINGUISHED THEOLOGIAN, GREETINGS FROM ERASMUS OF ROTTERDAM:

Your letter did not reach me, but a friend at Antwerp somehow or other obtained a copy and showed it to me. You lament the unfortunate publication of the *Folly*; you greatly approve of my work on the restoration of Jerome's text; you discourage me from editing the New Testament. Far from offending me, my dear Dorp, this letter of yours endears you even more, although you have always been a very dear friend. You have counseled me with such sincerity; you have admonished in such a friendly way; you have reproached me in such cordial fashion. Christian charity indeed has the ability to retain its own true sweetness even when it is exceedingly angry. I receive many letters daily from learned men, which hail me as the glory of Germany, which call me a great light—a sun, a moon—and heap upon me most brilliant titles which burden rather than adorn me. May I perish if I enjoyed any of them as much as that scolding letter from my friend Dorp. Paul rightly said that charity does not sin; it means to be of service, whether it flatters or whether it finds fault. Would that I had the leisure to answer your letter in a way that would satisfy so devoted a friend. I am most anxious to have your approval upon my work, because I prize so highly your magnificent talents, outstanding erudition, and keen judgment that I prefer to have the blessing of Dorp alone than that of a thousand others. And although I have until now been ill from my sea voyage, exhausted from traveling on horseback, and busy assembling my luggage, I thought it better to make some reply than to leave a friend in such an opinion of me, whether this be the result of your own evaluation or suggested by others who incited you to write this letter that they might act out their playlet behind another's mask.

First of all, to speak frankly, I almost regret publishing the *Folly*. That book won me no small amount of fame, or you might say, notoriety. Yet I care nought for fame if it is accompanied by envy. Heavens above! What is this whole thing called fame but an empty title bequeathed to us by pagan antiquity? Not a few words of this kind have lingered on among Christians until they call immortality the good name left to posterity and label as virtue any sort of devotion to letters. What I have aimed at in publishing all of my books was to serve some useful purpose through my efforts and, if I fell short of this, at least to avoid doing any harm to anyone. In like manner, although we see even great men misuse their writings to vent their own feelings, boasting of their silly love affairs, seducing people by flattery, using the pen to retaliate after an injury, blowing their own horns, outdoing a Thraso or a Purgopolinices,[5] I, though short in talent and with quite meagre learning, have always striven to do some good if possible; and when this were not possible,

[5] Thraso is a braggart in Terence's *Eunuchus*, and Purgopolinices the boastful hero of Plautus' *Miles gloriosus*.

at least I took care to injure no one. Homer indulged his
anger against Thersites, painting a vicious portrait of him
in his poetry. Plato took a great many people to task by
name in his dialogues. Aristotle spared no one, not even
Plato or Socrates. Demosthenes had his Aeschines against
whom he raged. Cicero had his Piso, his Vatinius, his Sal-
lust, his Antony. Seneca ridiculed quite a few people by
name. And if you consider more recent examples, the pen
was used as a weapon by Petrarch against a certain physician, by Valla against Poggio, by Poliziano against Scala.[6]
Where will you show me an author so moderate as not to
have written satirically against someone? Even Jerome, as
pious and serious a man as he was, sometimes was carried
away in anger at Vigilantius, is rather immoderate in his
insults to Jovinianus, inveighs against Rufinus with much
bitterness. It has always been the custom here for learned
men to commit to paper whatever they lament or take delight in, as if to trusted companions, and on this bosom to
pour out all their turbulent feelings. You even find some who
take up writing books with no other purpose save to fill
them with the passions of their own souls, which they
thereby pass on to posterity.

As for me, in the many books I published, I very openly
praised many a man but I never tarnished the reputation of
anyone. I never spilled the slightest stain on anyone. No race
of mankind, no profession, no individual did I ever censure
by name. If you only knew, my dear Dorp, how many times
I was really provoked to do this by such abuse as no one
should have tolerated! But I always overcame the tempta-
tion and considered that the impression left on posterity
was more important than giving these depraved men what
they deserved. If the facts were known to others just as
they were to me, men would think me not bitter but just, dis-

----

[6] Valla, Poggio, Poliziano, and Scala are all fifteenth-century Italian humanists.

passionate, yes, moderate. Also, I thought to myself: what interest will people have in my private feelings? or how will these affairs of mine be sufficiently familiar to readers far away or to posterity? I shall have dealt with my enemies in a manner worthy of myself, not in the manner they deserve. Besides, no one is so great an enemy that I would not want to turn him, if possible, into a friend. Why close the door on such a person? Why write against an enemy something which in some future time I might regret because that man has become my friend? Why should I ruin someone's reputation which I could not possibly restore even though he later on deserved it? I would rather err in this direction, namely, in giving praise to those who merit it not rather than in castigating those who are worthy. Whenever you praise someone mistakenly, it is attributed to simplicity, but if you even begin to paint in his true colors a man deserving ignominy, it is attributed not to his misdeeds but to your prejudice. Moreover, let us not forget that as a great war sometimes comes out of the avenging of injuries, so out of curses in turn hurled back and forth most perilous passions frequently are stirred. Just as it is hardly Christian to weigh injury against injury, so it is scarcely worthy of a stout heart to avenge hurts by shrieking like a woman.

For reasons such as this I have persuaded myself to guard my writings from any harmdoing or vengeance and to avoid contaminating them with so much as a mention of evil. Nor did I have any intentions in the *Folly* different from those in my other works, although the method may have differed. In the *Enchiridion* I simply set down a design for Christian living. In the pamphlet *The Education of a Prince* I publicly advised in what subjects a prince ought to be instructed. In the *Panegyric,* using the form of a eulogy of the prince, I did in an oblique manner the very same thing that in the other book I did openly and directly. So for the *Folly*; the same thing was done there under the semblance of a jest as was done in the *Enchiridion.* I wanted to admonish, not to cause pain; to be of benefit, not to vex; to reform the morals of men, not to oppose them. Plato the philosopher, grave as he is, approves of rather lavish drinking bouts among companions because he is of the opinion that certain vices can be dispelled by wine's laughter which cannot be corrected by severity. And Horace also thinks that an admonition that is jocose serves no less the purpose than one that is serious. "What is the matter," he says, "with saying the truth with a smile?"[7] The wise heads of old who preferred to present the salutary precepts of life in humorous and seemingly puerile fables had insight into a good principle, namely, that a truth of itself somewhat harsh, if presented in an entertaining fashion, more easily finds its way to men's hearts. Yes, this is the honey which in Lucretius the doctors smeared on the inside of the cup of absinthe for the treatment of children. It was for the same reason that the kings of old brought fools into their courts, that in the license given to such creatures certain little vices would be disclosed and corrected without offense to anyone. Perhaps it is not proper to put Christ in such a category. Yet if we can use certain comparisons between the divine and the human, did not His parables have something in common with the fables of the ancients? Evangelical truth sinks in more pleasingly and takes firmer hold in souls when dressed up in these little enticements than if it is simply stated as naked truth, an effect Augustine certainly strives for in his work on Christian doctrine. I observed continually how the common mass of humanity in every walk of life was being seduced by the most stupid opinions, and that the desire of a remedy was more genuine than the hope thereof. So it seemed to me justifiable to use a little deceit, as it were, on these pleasure-loving souls and give them their medicine disguised as pleasure. Again and again I had already seen this lively and playful kind of

[7] *Satires,* I, i, 24-25.

thing go a long way with many people. Now if you reply that the personage whom I invented for this purpose was too frivolous to serve as a spokesman in a discussion of serious matters, that fault I would perhaps admit. I do not object to the charge of a lapse of judgment, but I do object to the charge of having been bitter. Yet I could answer soundly even that first charge, if by no other means than citing the example of the very many important writers whom I listed in the preface of my book.

But how did I come to do this thing? I was staying for a while with my friend More after my return from Italy, and my kidney pains were confining me to the house for a few days. My collection of books was not yet delivered to me. And even if they had been brought, the illness did not permit the strain of any serious study anyway. So I began during my inactivity to play around with the idea of an encomium of Folly, not, of course, with the intention of publishing anything but rather to relieve the discomfort of my illness with this sort of relaxation.[8] I showed a little bit of the work I had begun to some friends, just to share the fun with someone and make it more amusing. Since they found great pleasure in it, they insisted that I continue. I yielded, and in this task I spent seven days, more or less, an expenditure of time which indeed seemed to exceed the value of the theme. Then, by the efforts of the very people under whose prompting I wrote it, the book was brought into France and set up in type, but from a copy that was not only faulty but even mutilated. As if this were not enough to make me unhappy about it, within a few months it was reprinted many times and in many different places. I wondered myself why it had such popularity.

If you call this a lapse of judgment, my dear Dorp, the

[8] In his Dedication to Thomas More of *The Praise of Folly,* Erasmus says that the idea came to him on the journey from Italy to England. Thinking of his good friend More, he was prompted to entertain himself with a eulogy of folly, More's name being very close to the Greek word for folly.

defendant pleads guilty or at least does not protest loudly. It was under these circumstances of my enforced leisure and in the desire to humor my friends that I committed a little indiscretion, and that once in a lifetime. But who is wise all the time? You yourself admit that my other writings are proper enough to be hailed by all pious and learned men. What censor, other than an Areopagite, is so strict that he is unwilling to pardon one single lapse of judgment in a writer? It is the last word in narrow-mindedness to forget the many times a writer was proper and circumspect and then, out of offense at one ridiculous little pamphlet, strip him of all honor. How many absurdities in other writers could I not mention, in many ways more absurd than this, even among great theologians, as they contrive quarrelsome and insipid questions and fight each other over the smallest trifles, as if defending house and home? These people without using masks put on performances more absurd than the Atellan farces. Certainly I am more worthy of respect in that, meaning deliberately to be a bit silly, I donned the mask of Foolishness, and, just as in Plato's home Socrates spoke the praises of love behind a veiled countenance, I acted out that little skit of mine using an appropriate mask.

You say that these men whom my work displeases praise my talent, erudition and eloquence but are offended by my reckless wit. Indeed these admonitors give me more credit than I would want. I certainly do not savor praise such as this, especially coming from men whom I consider to have neither talent nor erudition nor eloquence. If they had these qualities, my dear Dorp, believe me, they would not be so greatly offended by jokes that are more wholesome than they are erudite and ingenious. I beseech you by the Muses, what eyes, what ears, what palate do they have who have been offended by the sting in this little book? First of all, where is the sting when no one's name save my own has been damaged? They ought to bear in mind what Jerome frequently teaches: that when a discussion of vices is kept general, injury is done to no one, and if someone does take offense, he has no claim against the writer. If he wants to prefer charges, let him do so against himself, for he has betrayed himself by publicly applying to himself an assertion which was made in such general terms that it referred to no man in particular, unless someone chose to apply it to himself. You can observe that in the whole book I so restrained myself from mentioning names of individuals that I was unwilling to treat of a particular nation with more than a mild criticism. There is a place in the work where I single out a particular point of pride in each of the national groups. I attribute, for instance, to the Spanish an esteem for military prowess, to the Italians a love of letters and eloquence, to the English pride in a sumptuous table and in bodily beauty, and to other nations similar qualities which each could graciously acknowledge or at least hear with a smile. Then although in accordance with the plan of my work I treated of all social classes and dwelt on the vices of each and reprehended them, I never said anything that was foul or venomous. I never uncovered the cesspool of scandal. I never stirred up the secret Camarina of human life.[9] Anyone knows how much could have been said about bad pontiffs, unworthy bishops and priests, vicious princes, or for that matter about any rank or station in life, if only, like Juvenal, one did not blush from writing about the crimes many people do not blush from committing. They were pleasant things and laughable, not loathsome, deeds that I treated of, and I did it in such a way that I could slip in here and there a word of advice, sometimes on very serious matters. It is very important that my critics realize this.

I am sure you yourself do not have the time to engage in frivolities such as these. Nevertheless, if sometime you

[9] Camarina was a town in Sicily in ancient times, which had a stagnant and noisome pool near its walls.

have the leisure, give a little thought to those anecdotes in the *Folly*; surely you will find that they are more in the spirit of the teaching of the Evangelists and Apostles than are the so-called brilliant and masterful disputations conducted by certain people. Why, you yourself admit in your letter that many a truth is conveyed this way. Yet you think it was not expedient "to offend tender ears with the raw truth." If you think one ought under no circumstances to speak freely or that truth should never be proclaimed unless it offends no one, why do doctors treat patients with disagreeable medicines and rank the sacred bitters among the most praiseworthy remedies? Now if they do this in curing the diseases of the body, how much more seemly is it for us to do the same thing in healing the ills of the soul? "Reprove," says St. Paul, "entreat, rebuke, in and out of season."[10] The Apostle wants vice to be extirpated by every means possible, and you do not want so much as a sore to be touched, even when it is done with such moderation that no man could possibly be harmed unless he bring the harm upon himself. Actually, if there is any method at all of treating the ills of men without offending, this one, if I am not mistaken, is above all the best, namely, when not so much as a name of anyone appears and when caution is taken to refrain from anything that would offend pious ears. This point is well made because just as in tragedies there are certain things too atrocious to be exhibited before the eyes of the audience and it is found sufficient to narrate them, so in the habits of men there are some things more obscene than can be modestly portrayed. Finally, it is helpful to have the narration spoken by some kind of a ridiculous character with cracks and jokes, so that the good humor of the situation simply rules out any offense. Do we not see how even in the courts of cruel tyrants a joke is valued if it is suitable and spoken at the right moment? I ask you, what entreaty, what serious

10 2 Timothy 4:2.

rejoinder could have soothed the soul of the king in that famous story better than the jest of the soldier? "We were on the point," said the soldier, "of saying much more insulting things about you when the wine ran out." The king laughed and overlooked the offense. Nor was it without reason that the two rhetoricians, Cicero and Quintilian, gave such attention to the subject of laughter. Charm and an agreeable way of presenting things have such power that even when the apt phrase is turned against ourselves, we are delighted; witness the stories written about Julius Caesar. Wherefore, if you admit truth in what I wrote, if what I wrote is playful rather than offensive, what method more suitable could be devised for the treating of the common ills of mankind? Pleasure first invites the reader, and once he is caught up in the book, it makes him linger. Some seek this satisfaction, others that. Pleasure is bait for anyone and everyone, with the possible exception of one so dull-witted as to lack any taste for literature.

Those who are offended even though no one's name appears seem to me to be acting like touchy women who, if something is said against ladies of ill-repute, are disturbed as if such a reproach applied to all women. In like manner, if something praiseworthy is attributed to good women, they flatter themselves that what virtue one or other has redounds to the praise of all of them. Let this kind of absurdity be beneath men, and much more, learned men, and above all, theologians. If in this way I am charged with a fault of which I am innocent, I am not offended in the least; rather I congratulate myself if I am free of the faults of which I see many men guilty. But if the accusation has touched a sore spot and I see the mirror held up to myself, there still is no reason why I ought to take offense. If I am wise, I will hide my feelings and not betray myself. If I am without blemish, I will take caution at the admonition, lest at some time an attack like this should be directed at me personally

which I see now made without the mention of my name. Why
do we not make the same concessions to this little book
which even the ignorant *hoi polloi* make at popular plays?
How much abuse, and with what abandon, do they hurl at
monarchs, at priests, at monks, at wives, at husbands, and
at God-knows-whom? And yet because no one is attacked by
name, all laugh and each either candidly admits or prudently dissimulates his own foibles. Even the most irascible
tyrants bear with their jesters and fools when at times they
are smitten by them with an open insult. The Emperor
Flavius Vespasian did not take vengeance upon the fellow
who said he had the face of a person in the act of evacuat-
ing. Just who are these people of such delicate ear that they
cannot bear to hear lady Folly poke gentle fun at our common human condition without at the same time touching anyone in particular? The old-style comedy would never have
been driven off the stage had it abstained from mentioning illustrious people by name.

But you, good Dorp, write almost as if the book *Folly*
has alienated from me the whole theological profession.
"What was the need," you ask, "for lashing out so fiercely
at the theological profession?" And then you lament my unhappy position. "There was a time," you go on, "when all
read your writing with eagerness and hankered to meet you
in person. Now *Folly* like some Davus upsets all this." I
realize you write this in good faith, nor would I use a sub-
terfuge with you. I want to ask you if you really think the
whole theological profession has been attacked, if something was said against stupid and incompetent theologians
who were in fact unworthy of such a title? If such a rule
holds, the whole human race would consider itself offended
if anything were said against wicked men. What king was
ever so shameless as not to admit that some kings are bad
kings and not worthy of the title? What bishop was ever so
arrogant as not to admit the same for those in his state of

life? Are the theologians the only group which has not in its vast ranks a stupid, an ignorant, or a troublesome member, but has only Pauls, Basils and Jeromes to show us? Indeed, the contrary is the case; the more exalted any profession is, the fewer are the members who really measure up to it. You will find more good skippers than you will find good princes, more good physicians than good bishops. And this is nothing against the particular profession, but it is to the greater credit of those who in a brilliant profession perform brilliantly. I ask you now, tell me, why do theologians take greater offense (supposing there are some who are offended) than kings, than nobles, than magistrates, than bishops, than cardinals, than supreme pontiffs, or for that matter, than merchants, than husbands, than wives, than lawyers, than poets—for no species of the human race did Folly neglect—unless it is because these latter are not silly enough to take as said against themselves what was spoken against unworthy people in general. St. Jerome wrote to Eustochium on virginity and in this book exposed the morals of bad virgins as no Apelles could depict them. Was Eustochium offended? Was she enraged at Jerome because he cast disgrace upon virgins as a group? Not a bit of it! And why, in the last analysis? Because as a prudent virgin she would not consider it to refer to herself if something were said about bad virgins; on the contrary, she was glad to have the good virgins warned lest they degenerate into bad ones; she was glad also that bad ones were admonished to amend their ways. He wrote to Nepotian on the life of clerics. He wrote to Rusticus on the life of monks and painted them in vivid colors, but with equally marvelous acuteness he appraised the vices of both these states of life. Those to whom he wrote in no wise took offense because they knew none of these criticisms applied to them. Why was not William Mountjoy alienated, since he is prominent among the courtly aristocrats and *Folly* made great fun of the nobles of the court? I'll tell you why. Being an excellent and intelligent man, he thinks rightly that what is said against evil and ignorant nobles is not applicable to himself. *Folly* poked fun at bad and worldly bishops, too. Why was not the archbishop of Canterbury offended by this? Simply because as a man full of every virtue, he judged none of this applicable to himself.

Why should I go on recalling to you the names of the noblest princes, of other bishops, of abbots, of cardinals, of men renowned for their learning, among whom I feel no one has been alienated in the least bit from me because of my *Folly*? I cannot even be convinced that any of the theologians were irritated by this book, save perhaps some few who either are of little understanding or are envious or are of such critical disposition that they find no good in anything. As is well known, men of this high calling have in their ranks a certain few who have such poor talent and judgment that they are not capable of any kind of learning, much less theological learning. They learned by heart a few little rules from Alexander of Gaul;[11] in addition they mastered a little bit of silly sophistry; next they memorized ten propositions from Aristotle, I dare say without understanding them; then, from Scotus or Occam[12] they learned a like number of chapters; and whatever else they need know they rest content to draw it from the *Catholicon* or *Mammotrepton* or a similar dictionary, as if from some horn of plenty. Yet how they toss their heads in pride! Nothing is more arrogant than ignorance! These are the ones who condemn St. Jerome as a grammarian obviously because they do not understand him. Such men deride Greek, Hebrew, even

---

[11] Alexander of Gaul is a thirteenth-century writer who composed a Latin grammar for young students, the *Doctrinale puerorum*.

[12] Duns Scotus (d. 1308?) and William of Occam (d. 1349?) are two important scholastic philosophers and theologians. Erasmus had a particular dislike for the Scotist school. Occam is prominent in the development of medieval nominalism.

Latin; and even though they are more stupid than any pig
and lack common sense, they think they themselves occupy
the whole citadel of learning. They bring everyone to task;
they condemn; they pontificate; they are never in doubt; they
have no hesitations; they know everything. And yet few in
number as they are, these people are causing tremendous
commotion. What is more impudent, more obstinate than
ignorance! Such people are in one great conspiracy against
genuine learning. What they are doing is campaigning for
high rank among the theologians, and they are afraid lest,
if genuine learning should be born again and if the world
should return to its senses, they would appear to know nothing, whereas up to now people consider them omniscient.
From such as these come the complaints, from them all the
commotion, from them the conspiracy against men following the better scholarship. They do not like *Folly* because
they do not understand either Greek or Latin. If it is against
such theologians—I should rather say men who masquerade
as theologians—that something was said a bit critically,
what is it to that magnificent class of good theologians? If
these latter are motivated by a zeal for piety, why the prejudice against *Folly*? What impious, what foul, what perni-
cious stuff did Poggio write? But he is everywhere accepted
as a Christian author and translated into almost every
tongue.[13] With what abuse, with what imprecations did Pontano attack the clergy?[14] But he is read as charming and
amusing. What downright obscenity is there in Juvenal?
But some think him good to use in sermons. How offen-
sively did Tacitus write against the Christians, with what
hostility Suetonius? How impiously did Pliny and Lucian
scoff at the doctrine of the immortality of the soul? Yet all
read them for their erudition, and rightly so. The one thing

[13] The reference is to Poggio's obscene *Facetiae,* which had been translated
into English, French, Italian, and Spanish.

[14] Pontano is a fifteenth-century Italian humanist and poet.

they cannot stand is Lady Folly, just because she makes a few witty remarks, not about theologians who are good and deserving of that title, but against the frivolous quibblings of ignorant men and against the ridiculous title of *our master*.

Thus it is that two or three miserable fellows posing as theologians are trying to throw the weight of this odium on me, that I offended and made enemies of the whole theological profession. I have done this, I who give such a place to theological learning that I consider it the only true learning! Why, I so look up to and venerate the theologians that to their science alone, now or in the past, do I associate the name learning. Although modesty restrains me from assuming such an exalted title myself, I am nevertheless aware of what qualifications in learning and piety must accompany the name. I know of no greater profession for a man than that of theologian. That title is an adornment worthy of bishops, not of men like me. It is enough for me to have learned that saying of Socrates that we really do not know anything, and to have consequently devoted my efforts as far as possible to assisting the inquiries of other men. At all events, I am at a loss to know just who or where they are, those two or three gods among the theologians who, as you say, do not show themselves propitious to me. I have been around a bit since publishing the *Folly*; I have been at a lot of learned gatherings and in many a metropolis. Never did I sense that any theologian felt any wrath against me, except for one or other of their number who are hostile to all good scholarship. Nor did these latter ever remonstrate with me personally. What might be muttered behind my back I do not take much notice of, trusting as I do in the judgment of many good men. I am afraid I might seem more arrogant than honest in saying this, my dear Dorp, but really I can name for you many theologians, known for the sanctity of their lives, outstanding in learning, pre-eminent in dignity,

some of them even bishops, who never treated me with
greater affection than after the publication of the *Folly,*
and who liked the book better than I did myself. I would
mention each one of them here by name and title were I not
afraid that those three particular theologians would turn
their hostility against even such great men on account of the
Folly. I will go further and say that I suspect there is but one
author of all this disturbance—I can almost put the story
together by conjectures—and if I wanted to identify him,
no one would be surprised that the *Folly* displeased such a
man;[15] indeed, it would bother me if the book did not find
disfavor with such as he ; I too am dissatisfied with the
Folly. But on the other hand, the fact that it does not sit well
with such characters makes me a little less displeased with
it. What carries more weight with me is the judgment of
wise and learned theologians who not only refrain from beat-
ing me black and blue for my alleged bitterness, but praise
me to the skies for my moderation, even my candor, because,
although I am an impudent fellow by nature, I stop short
of impudence in my writing, and when I tease, I do so without inflicting injury. And now, in direct answer to those alone
whom I am supposed to have offended, look at how much
has been said even in public about the bad morals of some
theologians. The *Folly* does not engage in anything like
that. All it does is poke fun at their silly quibblings. It does
not even condemn the quibblings outright. It merely condemns those men who see in these quibblings the beginning
and end, the stem and stern, as it were, of the ship of theology, and who in their verbal wars, as St. Paul calls them, are
so engrossed that they have no time to read the Gospels, or
the Prophets, or the writings of the early Fathers. There
are all too many, my dear Dorp, guilty of this offense. I can

---

[15] Allen suggests (II, 100.373n) that this may be John Briard of Ath, but it
is possible that it is James Latomus, a sharp critic of Erasmus at this time and
later. Both were prominent Louvain theologians.

name you some past their eightieth birthday who wasted so much of their time in this nonsense that they never read the Gospel text, something they reluctantly admitted when it was pointed out by me.

Not even through the guise of my creature Folly did I dare to mention a complaint that I often hear people repeating, yes, people who are themselves theologians, and I mean real theologians, men of integrity, gravity, and learning and who drink deeply of the doctrine of Christ from its very fonts. These men, whenever they are among those to whom they can speak their minds freely, deplore this more recent brand of theology which has crept into the world, and long for the ancient one. What is holier, what more venerable, what can get right to the flavor and spirit of Christ's heavenly doctrine than the ancient theology? But this other type of theology, not to mention the base and monstrous nature of its crude, artificial style, its ignorance of good scholarship, and its ineptitude of expression, has been so adulterated by Aristotle, by trifling human inventions, and even by secular laws that I can hardly say it savors of the genuine and pure Christ. For it happens that when we fix too steadily on human traditions, we lose sight of the archetype. Hence, when the more prudent theologians are speaking in public, they are often forced to give a different account from what they would hold privately or would say to their friends. And often they may have no answer for those who question them when they realize that Christ taught one thing while petty human traditions demand another. What connection is there, I ask, between Christ and Aristotle? between the petty fallacies of logic and the mysteries of eternal wisdom? What is the purpose of this maze of disputations? How much of it is deadening and destructive by the very fact that it breeds contention and disagreement! Some problems, of course, should be investigated and others definitely settled; I quite agree. But on the other hand, there are many problems which it would be better to pass over than examine. Indeed, it is the part of wisdom to be ignorant of some things. There are many questions on which it is healthier to be in doubt than to be decided. Finally, if any decision has to be made, I would prefer that it be made with reverence and not arrogance, from the divine writings and not from the petty syllogisms fabricated by men. Now there is no end of these little questions, and yet how much discord there is on these very points among the sects and parties. Every day gives birth to a new decree. In brief, the result has been that matters of the greatest importance depend not on the law of Christ but on the definitions of scholastics and the power of some bishop. And the situation has been so hopelessly muddled that there is not even a hope of recalling the world to authentic Christianity. Men of the greatest piety and learning recognize and deplore these and many other conditions, and throw the principal blame for all of them on this bold and irreverent class of modern theologians.

Oh, dear Dorp, if you could read my innermost thoughts, you would clearly see how much I prudently conceal at this point. Of such the *Folly* makes no mention, or only a passing one, since I did not wish to offend anyone; and I have taken pains to preserve this same caution in all matters—not to write anything offensive, anything liable to destroy morality, anything seditious, or anything that could be construed as injurious to any class of society. Wherever I spoke about the cult of the saints, you will find in the passage an open assertion that nothing is being censured except the superstition of those who do not revere the saints properly. Similarly, if we say anything against princes, bishops, or monks, we always add the declaration that this was not written to injure the order itself, but against those who are corrupt and not worthy of their order, since I do not want to harm the good while I censure the vices of the wicked. And incidentally, while I am on the subject, I made it a point to mention no names, as far as possible, in order to avoid even offending the guilty. In short, in having the whole story told with wit and humor by a fictitious, amusing character, I was careful that even sad and sober people would find it agreeable.

Now you write that what I said is censured not for being satirical but for being impious. For, you say, how will pious ears take your calling the joys of the life to come a form of madness? My good Dorp, I beg you, tell me who taught a man of your openness to use this subtle sort of attack, or (as I tend to believe) what cunning person took advantage of your simplicity to spread this attack against me? This is the way those destructive critics usually work: they take a few words out of context, sometimes even changing them a little, omitting the facts which somehow soften and explain a harsh discourse. Quintilian in his *Institutes of Oratory* advocates this sort of tactic for presenting one's case in the best possible light: first give arguments, then add mitigating circumstances, extenuating circumstances, or whatever in any way helps the cause, but represent the arguments of the adversary unadorned by these devices and in the most offensive terms possible. These men of whom I speak did not learn their art from the precepts of Quintilian but from their own maliciousness. And that is why it often happens that words which would be quite agreeable if quoted as they were written, cause serious offense when they are repeated in another manner. Reread that section, I ask you, and consider carefully by what steps and what process of argumentation I arrived at the conclusion that this joy was a sort of madness. Further, look at the words I use to explain it. You will see there something which might even please pious ears, so far is it from being at all offensive. If there is any offense, it lies not in my book but in your rendering of it.

Indeed, while Folly was attempting to fix upon every class of being the label of foolishness and was teaching that the greatest human happiness depended on foolishness, every class of being was touched upon, right up to kings and supreme pontiffs. From these we came to the Apostles themselves and even to Christ, to whom we find attributed a folly of a sort in Sacred Scripture. But there is no danger at this point that anyone should imagine that Christ or the Apostles were really foolish; the point is that even they possessed some weakness and some likeness to our own passions which might make them appear lacking in wisdom when compared with that eternal and pure wisdom. But this very foolishness conquers all worldly wisdom, just as the Prophet compares the justice of all men to the wrappings of a woman soiled by the menstrual flow.[16] It is not that the justice of good men would be contaminated, but that whatever is purest in human eyes is in some ways impure when it is compared to the ineffable purity of God. And just as I declared foolishness wise, I consider madness sane and insanity prudent. In order to soften what I then said about the joy of holy people, I preface it with Plato's three forms of madness, the happiest being the madness of lovers, which is nothing else than a sort of ecstasy.[17] But the ecstasy of the pious is nothing but a foretaste of the happiness to come, by which we will be completely absorbed in God, destined to exist more in Him than in our very selves. Plato called it madness whenever anyone is swept outside himself, exists in what he loves, and enjoys it. Do you not see how carefully I distinguished shortly afterwards between the types of folly and insanity, so that no man, however simple, would be led astray by my words?

"But apart from the content," you say, "the very words will offend pious ears." Then why are those same pious ears not offended when they hear St. Paul saying "the folly of God" and "the folly of the cross?"[18] Why don't they

---

[16] Isaias 64:6.
[17] *Phaedrus*, 244–45.
[18] 1 Corinthians 1:25, 23.

call St. Thomas to account, since he wrote these words on St. Peter's ecstasy: "When, in a fit of pious foolishness, he began to talk about tents"?[19] He calls that holy and blessed rapture foolishness, and yet these very words are sung in the churches. Why didn't they call me to account in the past when once in a prayer I called Christ a magician and a charmer? St. Jerome calls Christ a Samaritan, even though He was a Jew. Paul calls the same Christ "sin," as if to say something worse than "sinner." He calls Christ accursed. What an irreverent insult, if anyone wanted to take it in the wrong sense; and what pious praise, if one takes it as Paul intended! For a similar example, if one calls Christ a thief, an adulterer, a drunkard, or a heretic, would not all good men refuse to listen? But if someone expresses this in appropriate words and gradually leads the reader by the hand through the course of his talk to the consideration of how Christ, triumphant on the cross, brought back to His Father a spoil redeemed from hell, how He took to Himself the synagogue of Moses like the wife of Uriah so that a peaceable people was born of it, how as one drunk with the new wine of charity He expended Himself for us, how He introduced a new doctrine, far removed from the commonplace utterances of both philosopher and ordinary man—who, I ask, could be offended, especially since we sometimes find in the sacred writings instances of these terms used in a good sense? In the *Chiliades* (since this happens to come to mind) I spoke of the Apostles as Sileni; indeed, I even called Christ a Silenus.[20] What would be more intolerable than if some hostile interpreter should come forward and superficially explain this in an offensive way? But let a pious and

---

[19] Perhaps *Commentarium in Mattheum* 17:5.

[20] Erasmus is referring to the essay *Sileni Alcibiadis* first published in the enlarged edition of the *Adagia* entitled *Proverbiorum chiliades* which Froben brought out in 1515. See M. M. Phillips, *The "Adages" of Erasmus* (Cambridge, 1964), pp. 271–73.

impartial person read what I wrote, and he will approve the allegory.

I am amazed, however, that these men have not noticed how cautiously I put these words and how eager I was to soften them by a correction. For I put it this way: "While I have on the lion skin, I will proceed to show that the happiness of Christians, which they seek with so much toil, is nothing but a kind of madness and folly. Do not take offense at these words; consider the argument instead."[21] Listen carefully. First, since Folly is treating such an obscure subject, I soften it with a proverb, saying that Folly has put on a lion skin. I do not simply say "madness and folly" but "a kind of madness and folly," so that you may understand that there is a pious folly and a blessed madness, according to the distinction I proceed to supply. Not satisfied with this, I add the words "kind of" to make it clear that there is an underlying metaphor and that it is not a simple statement. Not content with these distinctions, I beg them to excuse the offense the tone of the words might cause, and I warn them to pay more attention to what is said than to the words in which it is said. And indeed, I said this right in the very statement of my purpose. As a matter of fact, in the whole treatment of the subject, is there anything at all that is not said with piety and circumspection, and even with more reverence than would suit the role of Folly? In that section I preferred momentarily to neglect elegance rather than fail to do justice to the importance of the subject. I preferred offending rhetoric to wounding piety. And finally when the argument was completed, so that I would not offend anyone by having Folly, a humorous character, speak on a very sacred matter, I asked pardon for this fault with these very words: "But indeed I have long since forgotten who I am

---

[21] Erasmus, *The Praise of Folly*, trans. Leonard F. Dean (Chicago, 1946), p. 127.

and have run out of bounds. If anything I said seems too sharp or gossipy, remember that it is Folly and a woman who has spoken."[22]

You see that I continually forestalled any occasion for offense. But the people whose ears are attuned to nothing but propositions, conclusions, and corollaries, do not weigh sufficiently such matters. What about the preface in which I defended my book, where I try to forestall any criticism? I have no doubt that it was sufficient for all sincere men. But what would you do for those individuals who either do not want to be satisfied because of intellectual obstinacy or are too stupid to understand an apology? For just as Simonides said that the Thessalians were too dull to be deceived by him, so you should see that there are certain people who are too stupid to be able to be appeased. Moreover, it is not remarkable that they find something to criticize, since all they look for is something to criticize. If anyone should read the writings of St. Jerome in that spirit, he will find a hundred places which can easily be criticized; indeed, there are places in the most orthodox of Christian teachers which could be called heresy. I could say the same of Cyprian, Lactantius, and many others. Besides, who ever heard of bringing a humorous subject before the tribunal of the theologians? But if this is the rule, why don't they take the same pains to investigate everything written or trifled with by the poets of our day? How much offensive matter they will find there, how much that is redolent of ancient paganism! But since these writings are not considered serious, none of the theologians thinks they are any of his business.

Nevertheless, I would not demand that my case be supported by such examples. I would not want anything I wrote in jest to be in any way detrimental to Christian piety. Just give me a reader who understands what I wrote, who is fair and honest, who is eager for knowledge, and not bent on

[22] Ibid., p. 132.

criticism. If a writer would take into account this other class of readers—those first of all, who are endowed with no talent and less judgment, those, secondly, who had no training in literature and were spoiled rather than polished by base and confused learning, and those, finally, who are annoyed at anyone who knows what they are ignorant of and whose only aim is to criticize even what they might easily understand—this man surely would write nothing at all in his desire to avoid criticism. Why does the desire of glory impel these men to criticism? Because nothing is more vainglorious than ignorance joined with the conviction that one knows. Accordingly, since they ardently desire a good name and are not able to attain it by fair means, they prefer to imitate that young man from Ephesus who became famous by setting fire to the most celebrated temple in the world rather than live on in obscurity. And since they cannot produce anything worth reading, they apply themselves wholeheartedly to picking apart the works of famous men.

I speak of other men, not of myself, since I am completely insignificant. And I do not consider my book *Folly* worth a great deal, in case any of you might think that I am disturbed by this affair. What wonder that such men as I have described should choose a few statements and remove them from their context, make some of them out to be scandalous, some irreverent, some evil-sounding, and some savoring of impiety and heresy, not because they find these faults there, but because they bring them along themselves! How much more fitting and worthy of Christian simplicity it would be to support the activity of learned men and, if something happens to slip out thoughtlessly, to overlook it or interpret it favorably rather than maliciously to hunt for something to censure, acting like an informer and not a theologian! How much more felicitous it would be to teach or learn in mutual cooperation and, to use the words of Jerome, "to exercise on the playing-fields of learning without fear of incurring injury"! It is an amazing thing to see how there is no middle course for these men. They so read certain authors that they defend them on a trifling pretext, no matter how obvious it is that there is a mistake. They are so hostile to others that nothing can be said so circumspectly that they cannot criticize it on some ground. How much better, instead of doing what they are doing—wounding others and being wounded, wasting their own time and that of others—to learn Greek or Hebrew, or at least Latin, which are so indispensable to the knowledge of Sacred Scripture that I think it extremely impudent for anyone ignoring them to usurp the name of theologian!

Therefore, dear Martin, out of my good will toward you, I will not stop encouraging you, as I have done before, at least to add the knowledge of Greek letters to your studies. You have been exceptionally blessed in your talent; and your compact, bold, fluent, and luxuriant style gives evidence of not only a sound mind but also a prolific one. There is not only a full life ahead of you but one that is vigorous and productive as well. You have already completed the common course of studies with distinction. Believe me, if you add the summit of Greek letters to your very distinguished undertakings, I would dare to predict both to myself and others a great future for you and accomplishments not as yet equaled by any of the modern theologians. But if you hold the view that all human learning should be despised out of love for true piety, and that one arrives at this wisdom much more quickly through a certain transformation in Christ, and if it is your judgment that everything else worth learning can be seen more fully in the light of faith than in the books of men, I would gladly agree with your opinion. But if, as matters now stand, you promise yourself a true understanding of theology without a knowledge of languages and especially of that language in which the majority of the Divine Writings have been handed down, you have strayed far off the path.

And would that I were able to persuade you in this regard as well as I desire, for my desire is as great as my affection for you and my interest in your scholarly pursuits; and my affection is as strong as my interest is boundless. But if I am unable to make it entirely evident to you, I would like you at least to grant this favor to a friend's wishes—that you will make the attempt. I will decline no punishment if you do not finally agree that my advice was friendly and reliable. If my fondness for you means anything, if our common fatherland is at all important, if you put any value on what I would not dare to call my learning but certainly painstaking practice in literary endeavor, if you set any store by age (for I am old enough to be your father), promise me that you will do what I have asked of you, either out of favor or respect if not for logic's sake. So finally, if I convince you of this, I will think myself eloquent, as you always say I am. And if I succeed, both of us will rejoice: I because I gave the advice, you because you followed it. And now you who are the dearest to me of all will be still dearer because I have made you dearer to yourself. But if you do not agree now, I am afraid that when you are older and more experienced, you will approve my suggestion and condemn your own opinion. Then, as often happens, you will see your mistake when it is too late to correct it. I would be able to name for you a great number of men who, already gray-haired oldsters, were rejuvenated in the study of Greek, since they finally realized that without Greek the study of letters was feeble and groping.

But I have already said too much on this point. To return to your letter, you think there is but one way to assuage the ill will of the theologians and regain their former favor, that is, by way of a retraction, to set a *Praise of Wisdom* against the *Praise of Folly*. You earnestly urge and beg me to do this. My dear Dorp, since I disdain no one but myself and since I have a great desire to put all men at peace if possible, I would not hesitate to undertake this labor, if I did not foresee that whatever ill will has arisen among some few small-minded and stupid people would not only remain undiminished but would be even more inflamed. Therefore I think it better, as they say, to leave well enough alone and let sleeping dogs lie. Unless I am mistaken, this serpent will better fade away with time.

Now I come to another part of your letter. You wholeheartedly approve of my work in restoring Jerome, and you urge me on to similar labors. You are encouraging one who is already off to a start. Yet there is not as great a need for people to exhort me on to this work as there is for people to help me with it, so difficult is the task. But I would not want you to believe me in any regard henceforth, if you do not find me reliable on this point. Those whom the *Folly* seriously offends will not approve of this edition of Jerome either. Nor are they much more impartial to Basil, Chrysostom, Nazianzen than they are to me, except that they rage with less restraint against me, although in their wrath they sometimes are not afraid to hurl indignities at even these distinguished men. They fear good scholarship, and they are apprehensive for their absolute power. So that you may know that I am not making a rash prediction, no sooner had the work been started and the news spread abroad than some men of eminent reputation and some distinguished theologians—distinguished, at least, in their own opinion—came running to beg the printer by all that is sacred not to allow any Greek or Hebrew to get involved, saying that these languages were dangerous and possessed no value, being contrived only for curiosity's sake. Even before this time, while I was living in England, I happened to be having a cup of wine with a certain Franciscan, a Scotist of good repute, who seemed in the public eye to know a great deal and to know everything in his own. When I explained to him what I was attempting in Jerome, he was greatly astonished that there was anything in that man's writings that was not understood by the theologians. The man was so ignorant that I would be surprised if he really understood three verses in all Jerome's works. This good fellow added that, if I had any difficulties with the formulas of Jerome, there was a Breton who had written a splendid exposition on the whole subject.

I ask you, my dear Dorp, what can you do with such theologians? What would you pray for, except possibly a good doctor to cure their brains? And yet this is the sort of people who shout the loudest in the assembly of the theologians; and they are the men who decide the fate of Christianity. They fear and dread as though it were dangerous and destructive the very skill which St. Jerome and even aged Origen acquired for themselves at such great pains so that they might truly be theologians. Even Augustine, when he was an elderly bishop, lamented in his *Confessions* that as a young man he had shrunk from the study of those letters which would have been so useful in explaining Sacred Scripture. If there be any danger, I shall not fear the risk which men so wise have invited. If it is a curiosity, I do not want to be holier than Jerome; and let those very men who call what he did a curiosity see the service they do him.

There is extant a very old decree of the papal court on the appointment of instructors to teach certain languages publicly, whereas nowhere was any stipulation made on the teaching of sophistry or of Aristotle's philosophy, probably because the decrees call into question whether it is proper to teach these subjects or not. Besides, the study of these subjects is condemned by many renowned authors. Why do we neglect what the papal authority has ordered and embrace only that about which there is doubt, even disapproval? Yet the same difficulty meets these men in Aristotle as in Sacred Scripture. Everywhere they find that same Nemesis, avenger of the scorned language. They wander aimlessly, dream, strike out blindly, and produce nothing but monstrosities. We owe to these eminent theologians the fact that from the vast multitude of writers whom Jerome catalogued, such a small number survive, since *our masters* could not understand what they wrote. They are also to blame for the fact that St. Jerome's text is so maimed and distorted that those who try to re-edit it have almost as much trouble as Jerome himself had in writing it.

Now indeed, when in the third place you write regarding the New Testament, I wonder what has happened to you or whither your judgment so astute has in the meantime wandered. You do not want me to change anything except where there might be, perhaps, a little clearer meaning in the Greek. You deny that there are faults in the edition we commonly use, and you think that we are forbidden to alter in any way something approved by the agreement of so many ages and so many synods. I ask you, most learned Dorp, if what you write is true, why is it that Jerome, Augustine, and Ambrose had different readings from the ones that we have? Why did Jerome expressly censure and correct many readings which are still contained in this edition? What will you do in the face of such converging testimony, that is, when the Greek codices offer a different reading from ours, when Jerome in making citations uses that reading, when the most ancient Latin texts have the same reading, when its meaning fits better into the context? Are you going to disregard all these facts and still follow your own codex, which might have been corrupted by a copyist? Certainly no one is stating that there are mistakes in the Divine Writings (something you seemed to have suggested); nor is there any question here of that dispute Augustine had with Jerome. The solution to the problem almost stares us in the face, for it would be clear even to a blind man, as they say, that the Greek was often poorly translated because of the ignorance or laziness of a translator, that often the authentic and true text has been corrupted by ignorant copyists (something we see happening every day) or even changed by unskilled or inattentive ones. Who is more indulgent to error: the one who corrects and restores the mistakes, or the one who would sooner see a blunder added than removed, especially since it is the nature of mistakes that one causes another? And what we are changing is of such a nature that the corrections are concerned more with the tone of a passage than with its meaning, although the tone often constitutes a large part of meaning. But it is not seldom that there is a total deviation. And whenever this happens, to what, I ask you, do Augustine, Hilary, and Jerome have recourse but to the Greek sources? Although this practice has been approved even by ecclesiastical decrees, you still hedge and attempt to refute it, or rather evade it with a petty distinction.

You write that in that day the Greek codices had been emended more than the Latin ones, but that now it is just the opposite and that moreover we should not rely on the writings of those who fell away from the Roman Church. I can hardly bring myself to believe that you are really sincere in writing this. What are you saying? Shall we not read the writings of people who fell away from the Christian faith? Why, then, do they give such authority to Aristotle, a pagan who never had anything to do with the faith? The whole Jewish race severed itself from Christ; will the Psalms and the Prophets have no importance in our eyes, since they were written in Hebrew? Enumerate all the points on which the Greeks disagree with orthodox Latins: you will find nothing which has come from the words of the New Testament or which is relevant here. The whole controversy is about the word "hypostatic," about the procession of the Holy Spirit, about the rites of consecration, about the poverty of priests, about the authority of the Roman pontiff. And on none of these points do the Greeks try to prove their claims from falsified texts. And what will you say when you see that Origen, Chrysostom, Basil, and Jerome have explained passages in identical ways? Did someone in their time also falsify the Greek codices? Or who at any time ever discovered the Greek codices altered in even one spot? Finally, why would the Greeks want to interpolate, since they did not defend their doctrines from the text? Add to this the fact that even Cicero admits that the Greek codices were generally more correct than ours in every branch of learning, even though he is rather harsh on the Greeks in other respects. Indeed the separation of the letters, the forms of the letters, and the very strangeness of the script are reasons why the text could not be so easily corrupted or, if some mistake were made, it would be easier to restore the text.

Besides, when you write that we should not put aside our present edition after it has been clearly approved by so many councils, you are acting like the commonplace theologians who are wont to attribute to ecclesiastical authority whatever in any way has crept into public usage. Quote for me even one synod in which this edition was approved. For who could have approved something whose author was unknown? Jerome's preface states that it is not his own. But let us suppose that some synod did approve it. Did it approve it in such a way that we are not allowed to emend it from the Greek sources at all? Did it also approve all the faults which in various ways could have crept into the text? Was the decree of the Fathers formulated in the following words: "We do not know the author of this edition, but nevertheless we approve it. We do not want anything changed, even if the Greek codices are different, no matter how correct they are, even if Chrysostom, Athanasius, or Jerome had a different reading, even if this reading would square better with the evangelical sense, although we have highly approved these very authors in other instances. Further still, we approve by the same authority whatever will have been in the future falsified, corrupted, added, or omitted in any way by undertrained and over-confident copyists or by unskilled, drunken, and negligent ones. We do not want to permit anyone to change a single passage once it has been introduced"? A ridiculous decree, you would say. But it necessarily has to be so, if you would discourage me from my undertaking by the authority of a synod.

Finally, what are we to say when we see that the copies of this edition do not even agree? Did the synod also approve these inconsistencies with the foreknowledge, perhaps, of what changes would be made in each? My dear Dorp, would that the Roman pontiff had enough time to put into effect proper constitutions concerning these matters, in which care might be taken to restore the writings of these authors and to prepare and restore the texts which had been emended. But I would not want these men, by a misnomer called theologians, to sit on this council, these men whose sole aim has been to see that what they have learned should prevail. What did they ever learn that was not most absurd and completely confused? If decision falls to these tyrants, the better authors of antiquity will be rejected and the world will be forced to consider as from oracles their insipid incantations. Their writings possess so little good learning that had I no better training than they, I would rather be an ordinary craftsman than the best man of their class. They are the men who would not want anything restored lest they appear to be ignorant of something. They throw up at us the fictitious authority of councils; they exaggerate the great split in the Christian faith and the dangers to the Church (whose weight they are evidently supporting on their shoulders, whereas they would be better suited to pulling wagons), and they spread other grave warnings among the ignorant and superstitious people. Since they are known among these people as theologians, they thus wish to guard their reputation from damage. They fear that when they cite Sacred Scripture erroneously, as they often do, the authority of Greek or Hebrew truth will be thrown in their faces, and what was thought to be an oracle would soon be clearly seen to be a revery. St. Augustine, a great man and a bishop at the time, was not reluctant to learn even from a year-old boy. Men of their sort would rather turn the world upside down than be forced to admit that they are ignorant of anything that an educated man should know. Yet I see nothing here that particularly involves the purity of the Christian faith, but if such a thing were at stake, this would surely be all the more reason to redouble our efforts.

There is no danger that anyone will immediately desert Christ if he happens to hear that in the sacred books an unskilled or drowsy copyist corrupted something or that some unknown translator made a poor rendition. This danger springs from other causes, which I prudently pass over here. How much more Christian it would be to put aside all conflict and bring forward with good spirit whatever is of advantage for the common good, learning what you do not know without pride and teaching what you do know without jealousy. But if they are too uneducated to be able to teach anything correctly or too proud to learn anything, let them go their way, since there are only a few of them, and let us turn our attention to minds which are either good or promising. I once showed some of my notes which were in a rough draft, still hot from the anvil, as they say, to certain men of utmost impartiality, among whom were renowned theologians and learned bishops. They admitted that from such rough notes a great deal of light had been shed on the understanding of the Divine Writings.

I was quite aware of what you told me concerning Lorenzo Valla, that he had already taken up this task before me.[23] As a matter of fact, I was the first one to publish his notes; and I have also seen the commentaries of Jacques Lefèvre on the Pauline Epistles.[24] Would that these men had so elaborated the subject that there would be no need for my labors. Certainly I consider Valla deserving of the highest praise; he was a rhetorician more than a theologian, who had the diligence in treating of Sacred Scripture to compare the Greek with the Latin, although there are not many theologians who have read the Bible from cover to cover. Yet I disagree with him in a number of places, especially in those which have theological implications. As for Jacques Lefèvre, he was still at work on his commentaries when I set about my undertaking; and it is unfortunate that it did not occur to either of us to mention his work to the other even in our intimate conversations. I did not even know what he was about until he brought the work out in published form. I approve his endeavor wholeheartedly. Nevertheless, I disagree with him on some points, regretfully so, because I would gladly be in total agreement with such a good friend, except that more account should be shown truth than friendship, especially in the case of Sacred Scripture.

Still, the reason why you bring these two men to my attention is not sufficiently clear. Are you trying to discourage me from the subject as though it were already pre-empted? But we will see that I have not undertaken this task without reason, even though in the wake of such esteemed men. Or do you mean that theologians do not approve of the work of these two? I do not see what this would add to

[23] See Selection II, note 8.
[24] Jacques Lefèvre d'Étaples (1455–1536) was the great French biblical humanist whose work in many ways parallels that of Erasmus. His edition of and commentary on St. Paul's Epistles appeared in 1512. See also Selection I, note 13. On Lefèvre, see Augustin Renaudet, *Humanisme et Renaissance* (Geneva, 1958), pp. 201 ff.

Lorenzo's old unpopularity. I hear Lefèvre being praised by everyone. And how can you say theirs is the exact task I am undertaking? Lorenzo merely commented on a few passages and that, as it appears, in a very cursory and, as is said, superficial manner. Lefèvre published commentaries only on the Pauline Epistles, translating them after his own fashion, and if there were any difficulties, he merely noted them as they occurred. I have translated the entire New Testament according to the Greek original, with the Greek appended directly to allow for quicker comparison. I added notes separately in which, partly by proofs and partly by the authority of early theologians, I show that what I emended was not changed rashly, lest my corrections should lack credence or my emendations be easily altered. Would that I had been able to accomplish what I tried so hard to do! As far as the Church is concerned, I will have no fears in dedicating my work to any bishop, cardinal, or even Roman pontiff, provided he be like the present one.[25] Finally, I have no doubt that you too will offer your congratulations when the book has been printed, even though you are now trying to discourage me from publishing it, provided you become somewhat acquainted with that language without which it would be impossible to appraise the matter correctly.

See, my dear Dorp, how by one and the same work you have performed a twofold service: one you have performed for the theologians whose views you so carefully represented, and another you have performed for me, to whom you have more clearly manifested your affection by your friendly correction. You, in turn, should take in good part my equally unrestrained explanation. And if you are wise, you will assent more to my advice than to the advice of those men, who are eager to draw into their faction your genius, which is so promising, solely for the purpose of

[25] Erasmus did dedicate his New Testament to the pope then reigning, Leo X.

strengthening their forces by gaining a leader. Let them pursue better ends if they can; but if they take a poorer course, you must still follow the best one. And if you are not able to better them—which I would want you to strive for—at least be careful that they do not corrupt you. Hence I beg you to plead my case with them just as loyally as you pleaded their cause with me. Endeavor to put these fellows at peace as far as possible and convince them that what I am doing is not intended to insult those who are unfamiliar with this scholarship, but that it is meant to serve the common good. This explanation will suffice for those who are disposed to accept it but will convince no one who prefers to reject it. Then add that I am so minded that should anyone arise who would or could teach a better doctrine, I would be the first to retract my opinions and subscribe to his point of view.

Extend my cordial regards to John Paludanus, and see to it that you bring him in on this controversy over *Folly* by reason of the commentaries dedicated to him by our friend Lister.[26] Please commend me earnestly to the learned Nevius, and to the cultured Nicholas of Beveren, provost of St. Peter's.[27] I admire and revere for your sake Abbot Menardus, whom you praise so highly;[28] I have no doubt the praise is deserved, since you are trustworthy; and I do not forget to mention him very honorably in my letters whenever there is a fitting occasion. Health and farewell, Dorp, dearest of men.

Antwerp, 1515

[26] John Paludanus was a professor of oratory at Louvain and a close friend of Erasmus. Gerard Lister, a former student of Paludanus, annotated *The Praise of Folly* for the edition published by Froben in early 1515.

[27] Nevius was the principal of the Collège du Lis at Louvain. Nicholas of Beveren, provost of St. Peter's church at Utrecht, was a member of the noble house of Veere and Beveren. He was living in Louvain at this time.

[28] Menardus, abbot of the Benedictine Abbey at Egmond, was a close friend and patron of Dorp.

IV

The *Paraclesis*

The *Paraclesis* is the preface to Erasmus' Greek and Latin edition of the New Testament, which Froben first published in February 1516.[1] The word itself is Greek and means a summons or exhortation. In this context it is a summons or exhortation to the Christian to study Holy Scripture, where alone he will find the teachings of Christ in all their fullness and life. These incomparable writings, Erasmus declares in his concluding words, "bring you the living image of His holy mind and the speaking, healing, dying, rising Christ Himself, and thus they render Him so fully present that you would see less if you gazed upon Him with your very eyes."

The *Paraclesis* is one of the great classic statements of Erasmus' biblical humanism.[2] Its argument is simple and somewhat repetitive, and the essay, as important as it is, would seem to have been written in haste. Yet it is a moving and even powerful document, and it expresses as well as any other single work the religious ideals of Erasmus. There is frequent use and a definition in it of the famous Erasmian term "the philosophy of Christ." It also contains the oft-quoted passage of Erasmus wherein he hopes that Holy Scripture will be translated into the vernacular and be read by all and that the farmer and the weaver will sing verses from it at their work.

[1] The Latin text is in *Desiderius Erasmus Roterdamus: Ausgewählte Werke,* ed. Hajo Holborn (Munich, 1933), pp. 139–49. The present translation was made by the editor from the Holborn edition. The only other English translation, in so far as the editor knows, is a rather quaint early one attributed to William Roy and published at Marburg in Hesse in 1529.

[2] For appraisals of the *Paraclesis,* see M. M. Phillips, *Erasmus and the Northern Renaissance* (London, 1949), pp. 77–85, and Jacques Etienne, *Spiritualisme érasmien et théologiens louvanistes* (Louvain, 1956), pp. 18–22.

The illustrious Lactantius Firmianus, good reader, whose
eloquence Jerome especially admires, as he begins to defend
the Christian religion against the pagans desires especially
an eloquence second only to Cicero's be given him, thinking
it wrong, I believe, to want an equal eloquence.[3] But I indeed might heartily wish, if anything is to be gained by
wishes of this kind, so long as I exhort all men to the most
holy and wholesome study of Christian philosophy and summon them as if with the blast of a trumpet, that an eloquence far different from Cicero's be given me: an eloquence
certainly much more efficacious, if less ornate than his. Or
rather [I might wish for that kind of eloquence], if such
power of speech was ever granted anyone, as the tales of the
ancient poets not entirely without cause attributed to Mer-
cury, who as if with a magic wand and a divine lyre induces
sleep when he wishes and likewise snatches sleep away,
plunging whom he wished into hell and again calling them
forth from hell; or as the ancient tales assigned to Amphion
and Orpheus, one of whom is supposed to have moved hard
rocks, the other to have attracted oaks and ashes with a
lyre; or as the Gauls ascribed to their Ogmius, leading about
whither he wished all men by little chains fastened to their
ears from his tongue; or as fabled antiquity attributed to
Marsyas; or really, lest we linger too long on fables, as
Alcibiades imputed to Socrates and old comedy to Pericles,
an eloquence which not only captivates the ear with its fleeting delight but which leaves a lasting sting in the minds of
its hearers, which grips, which transforms, which sends away
a far different listener than it had received. One reads that
the noble musician Timotheus, singing Doric melodies, was
wont to rouse Alexander the Great to a desire for war. Nor
were they lacking in former times who considered nothing

[3] Lactantius Firmianus was an early fourth-century Christian writer, the
author of a defense of the Christian faith entitled *Institutiones divinae*. He
had a reputation for great eloquence.

more effective than the entreaties which the Greeks call
epodes. But if there were any such kind of incantation anywhere, if there were any power of song which truly could
inspire, if any Pytho truly swayed the heart, I would desire
that it be at hand for me so that I might convince all of the
most wholesome truth of all. However, it is more desirable
that Christ Himself, whose business we are about, so guide
the strings of our lyre that this song might deeply affect and
move the minds of all, and, in fact, to accomplish this there
is no need for the syllogisms and exclamations of the orators. What we desire is that nothing may stand forth with
greater certainty than the truth itself, whose expression is
the more powerful, the simpler it is.

And in the first place it is not pleasing to renew at the
present time this complaint, not entirely new but, alas, only
too just—and perhaps never more just than in these days—
that when men are devoting themselves with such ardent
spirit to all their studies, this philosophy of Christ alone is
derided by some, even Christians, is neglected by many, and
is discussed by a few, but in a cold manner (I shall not say
insincerely). Moreover, in all other branches of learning
which human industry has brought forth, nothing is so
hidden and obscure which the keenness of genius has not
explored, nothing is so difficult which tremendous exertion
has not overcome. Yet how is it that even those of us who
profess to be Christian fail to embrace with the proper
spirit this philosophy alone? Platonists, Pythagoreans, Aca-
demics, Stoics, Cynics, Peripatetics, Epicureans not only
have a deep understanding of the doctrines of their respec-
tive sects, but they commit them to memory, and they fight
fiercely in their behalf, willing even to die rather than abandon the defense of their author. Then why do not we evince
far greater spirit for Christ, our Author and Prince? Who
does not judge it very shameful for one professing Aristotle's philosophy not to know that man's opinion about the

causes of lightning, about prime matter, about the infinite?
And neither does this knowledge render a man happy, nor
does the lack of it render him unhappy. And do not we,
initiated in so many ways, drawn by so many sacraments to
Christ, think it shameful and base to know nothing of His
doctrines, which offer the most certain happiness to all? But
what purpose is served to exaggerate the matter by controversy, since it is what I might call a kind of wicked madness to wish to compare Christ with Zeno or Aristotle and
His teaching with, to put it mildly, the paltry precepts of
those men? Let them magnify the leaders of their sect as
much as they can or wish. Certainly He alone was a teacher
who came forth from heaven, He alone could teach certain
doctrine, since it is eternal wisdom, He alone, the sole
author of human salvation, taught what pertains to salvation, He alone fully vouches for whatsoever He taught, He
alone is able to grant whatsoever He has promised. If anything is brought to us from the Chaldeans or Egyptians, we
desire more eagerly to examine it because of the fact that it
comes from a strange world, and part of its value is to have
come from far off; and oftentimes we are anxiously tormented by the fancies of an insignificant man, not to say an
impostor, not only to no avail but with great loss of time
(I am not adding a more serious note, for the matter as it
stands is most serious). But why does not such a desire also
excite Christian minds who are convinced—and it is a fact
—that this teaching has come not from Egypt or Syria but
from heaven itself? Why do not all of us ponder within
ourselves that this must be a new and wonderful kind of
philosophy since, in order to transmit it to mortals, He who
was God became man, He who was immortal became mortal,
He who was in the heart of the Father descended to earth?
It must be a great matter, and in no sense a commonplace
one, whatever it is, because that wondrous Author came to
teach after so many families of distinguished philosophers,

after so many remarkable prophets. Why, then, out of pious curiosity do we not investigate, examine, explore each tenet? Especially since this kind of wisdom, so extraordinary that once for all it renders foolish the entire wisdom of this world, may be drawn from its few books as from the most limpid springs with far less labor than Aristotle's doctrine is extracted from so many obscure volumes, from those huge commentaries of the interpreters at odds with one another— and I shall not add with how much greater reward. Indeed, here there is no requirement that you approach equipped with so many troublesome sciences. The journey is simple, and it is ready for anyone. Only bring a pious and open mind, possessed above all with a pure and simple faith. Only be docile, and you have advanced far in this philosophy. It itself supplies inspiration as a teacher which communicates itself to no one more gladly than to minds that are without guile. The teachings of the others, besides the fact that they give hope of a false happiness, drive off the natural talents of many by the very difficulty, it is clear, of their precepts. This doctrine in an equal degree accommodates itself to all, lowers itself to the little ones, adjusts itself to their measure, nourishing them with milk, bearing, fostering, sustaining them, doing everything until we grow in Christ. Again, not only does it serve the lowliest, but it is also an object of wonder to those at the top. And the more you shall have progressed in its riches, the more you shall have withdrawn it from the shadow of the power of any other. It is a small affair to the little ones and more than the highest affair to the great. It casts aside no age, no sex, no fortune or position in life. The sun itself is not as common and accessible to all as is Christ's teaching. It keeps no one at a distance, unless a person, begrudging himself, keeps himself away.

Indeed, I disagree very much with those who are unwilling that Holy Scripture, translated into the vulgar tongue, be read by the uneducated, as if Christ taught such intricate doctrines that they could scarcely be understood by very few theologians, or as if the strength of the Christian religion consisted in men's ignorance of it. The mysteries of kings, perhaps, are better concealed, but Christ wishes his mysteries published as openly as possible. I would that even the lowliest women read the Gospels and the Pauline Epistles. And I would that they were translated into all languages so that they could be read and understood not only by Scots and Irish but also by Turks and Saracens. Surely the first step is to understand in one way or another. It may be that many will ridicule, but some may be taken captive. Would that, as a result, the farmer sing some portion of them at the plow, the weaver hum some parts of them to the movement of his shuttle, the traveller lighten the weariness of the journey with stories of this kind! Let all the conversations of every Christian be drawn from this source. For in general our daily conversations reveal what we are. Let each one comprehend what he can, let him express what he can. Whoever lags behind, let him not envy him who is ahead; whoever is in the front rank, let him encourage him who follows, not despair of him. Why do we restrict a profession common to all to a few? For it is not fitting, since Baptism is common in an equal degree to all Christians, wherein there is the first profession of Christian philosophy, and since the other sacraments and at length the reward of immortality belong equally to all, that doctrines alone should be reserved for those very few whom today the crowd call theologians or monks, the very persons whom, although they comprise one of the smallest parts of the Christian populace, yet I might wish to be in greater measure what they are styled. For I fear that one may find among the theologians men who are far removed from the title they bear, that is, men who discuss earthly matters, not divine, and that among the monks who profess the poverty of Christ and the contempt of the world you may find something more than worldliness. To me he is truly a theologian who teaches not by skill with intricate syllogisms but by a disposition of mind, by the very expression and the eyes, by his very life that riches should be disdained, that the Christian should not put his trust in the supports of this world but must rely entirely on heaven, that a wrong should not be avenged, that a good should be wished for those wishing ill, that we should deserve well of those deserving ill, that all good men should be loved and cherished equally as members of the same body, that the evil should be tolerated if they cannot be corrected, that those who are stripped of their goods, those who are turned away from possessions, those who mourn are blessed and should not be deplored, and that death should even be desired by the devout, since it is nothing other than a passage to immortality. And if anyone under the inspiration of the spirit of Christ preaches this kind of doctrine, inculcates it, exhorts, incites, and encourages men to it, he indeed is truly a theologian, even if he should be a common laborer or weaver. And if anyone exemplifies this doctrine in his life itself, he is in fact a great doctor. Another, perhaps, even a non-Christian, may discuss more subtly how the angels understand, but to persuade us to lead here an angelic life, free from every stain, this indeed is the duty of the Christian theologian.

But if anyone objects that these notions are somewhat stupid and vulgar, I should respond to him only that Christ particularly taught these rude doctrines, that the Apostles inculcated them, that however vulgar they are, they have brought forth for us so many sincerely Christian and so great a throng of illustrious martyrs. This philosophy, unlettered as it appears to these very objectors, has drawn the highest princes of the world and so many kingdoms and peoples to its laws, an achievement which the power of tyrants and the erudition of philosophers cannot claim. Indeed I do not object to having that latter wisdom, if it

seems worthwhile, discussed among the educated. But let
the lowly mass of Christians console themselves certainly
with this title because, whether the Apostles knew or other
Fathers understood these subtleties or not, they surely didn't
teach them. If princes in the execution of their duties would
manifest what I have referred to as a vulgar doctrine, if
priests would inculcate it in sermons, if schoolmasters would
instill it in students rather than that erudition which they
draw from the fonts of Aristotle and Averroës, Christendom would not be so disturbed on all sides by almost con-
tinuous war, everything would not be boiling over with such
a mad desire to heap up riches by fair means or foul, every
subject, sacred as well as profane, would not be made to
resound everywhere with so much noisy disputation, and,
finally, we would not differ from those who do not profess
the philosophy of Christ merely in name and ceremonial.
For upon these three ranks of men principally the task of
either renewing or advancing the Christian religion has been
placed: on the princes and the magistrates who serve in
their place, on the bishops and their delegated priests, and
on those who instruct the young eager for all knowledge.
If it happen that they, having laid aside their own affairs,
should sincerely cooperate in Christ, we would certainly see
in not so many years a true and, as Paul says, a genuine race
of Christians everywhere emerge, a people who would restore the philosophy of Christ not in ceremonies alone and
in syllogistic propositions but in the heart itself and in the
whole life. The enemies of the Christian name will far more
quickly be drawn to the faith of Christ by these weapons
than by threats or arms. In the conquest of every citadel
nothing is more powerful than the truth itself. He is not a
Platonist who has not read the works of Plato; and is he a
theologian, let alone a Christian, who has not read the literature of Christ? Who loves me, Christ says, keeps my word,
a distinguishing mark which He himself prescribed. There-

fore, if we are truly and sincerely Christian, if we truly
believe in Him who has been sent from Heaven to teach us
that which the wisdom of the philosophers could not do, if
we truly expect from Him what no prince, however powerful, can give, why is anything more important to us than His
literature? Why indeed does anything seem learned that is
not in harmony with His decrees? Why in the case of this
literature that should be revered do we also allow ourselves,
and I shall say almost to a greater extent than do the secular
interpreters in the case of the imperial laws or the books of
the physicians, to speak whatever comes to mind, to distort,
to obscure? We drag heavenly doctrines down to the level
of our own life as if it were a Lydian rule, and while we
seek to avoid by every means appearing to be ignorant and
for this reason gather in whatever is of account in secular
literature, that which is of special value in Christian philosophy I shall not say we corrupt, but—and no one can deny it
—we restrict to a few, although Christ wished nothing to be
more public. In this kind of philosophy, located as it is more
truly in the disposition of the mind than in syllogisms, life
means more than debate, inspiration is preferable to erudition, transformation is a more important matter than intellectual comprehension. Only a very few can be learned, but
all can be Christian, all can be devout, and—I shall boldly
add—all can be theologians.

Indeed, this philosophy easily penetrates into the minds
of all, an action in especial accord with human nature. Moreover, what else is the philosophy of Christ, which He himself calls a rebirth, than the restoration of human nature
originally well formed? By the same token, although no one
has taught this more perfectly and more effectively than
Christ, nevertheless one may find in the books of the pagans
very much which does agree with His teaching. There was
never so coarse a school of philosophy that taught that
money rendered a man happy. Nor has there ever been one

so shameless that fixed the chief good in those vulgar honors and pleasures. The Stoics understood that no one was wise unless he was good; they understood that nothing was truly good or noble save real virtue and nothing fearful or evil save baseness alone. According to Plato, Socrates teaches in many different ways that a wrong must not be repaid with a wrong, and also that since the soul is immortal, those should not be lamented who depart this life for a happier one with the assurance of having led an upright life. In addition, he teaches that the soul must be drawn away from the inclinations of the body and led to those which are its real objectives although they are not seen. Aristotle has written in the *Politics* that nothing can be a delight to us, even though it is not in any way despised, except virtue alone. Epicurus also acknowledges that nothing in man's life can bring delight unless the mind is conscious of no evil, from which awareness true pleasure gushes forth as from a spring. What shall we say of this, that many—notably Socrates, Diogenes, and Epictetus—have presented a good portion of His teaching? But since Christ both taught and presented the same doctrine so much more fully, is it not a monstrous thing that Christians either disregard or neglect or even ridicule it? If there are things that belong particularly to Christianity in these ancient writers, let us follow them. But if these alone can truly make a Christian, why do we consider them as almost more obsolete and replaced than the Mosaic books? The first step, however, is to know what He taught; the next is to carry it into effect. Therefore, I believe, anyone should not think himself to be Christian if he disputes about instances, relations, quiddities, and formalities with an obscure and irksome confusion of words, but rather if he holds and exhibits what Christ taught and showed forth. Not that I condemn the industry of those who not without merit employ their native intellectual powers in such subtle discourse, for I do not wish anyone to be offended, but that I think, and rightly so, unless I am mistaken, that that pure and genuine philosophy of Christ is not to be drawn from any source more abundantly than from the evangelical books and from the Apostolic Letters, about which, if anyone should devoutly philosophize, praying more than arguing and seeking to be transformed rather than armed for battle, he would without a doubt find that there is nothing pertaining to the happiness of man and the living of his life which is not taught, examined, and unraveled in these works. If we desire to learn, why is another author more pleasing than Christ himself? If we seek a model for life, why does another example take precedence for us over that of Christ himself? If we wish some medicine against the troublesome desires of the soul, why do we think the remedy to be more at hand somewhere else? If we want to arouse a soul that is idle and growing listless by reading, where, I ask, will you find sparks equally alive and efficacious? If the soul seems distracted by the vexations of this life, why are other delights more pleasing? Why have we steadfastly preferred to learn the wisdom of Christ from the writings of men than from Christ himself? And He, since He promised to be with us all days, even unto the consummation of the world, stands forth especially in this literature, in which He lives for us even at this time, breathes and speaks, I should say almost more effectively than when He dwelt among men. The Jews saw and heard less than you see and hear in the books of the Gospels, to the extent that you make use of your eyes and ears, whereby this can be perceived and heard.

And what kind of a situation is this, I ask? We preserve the letters written by a dear friend, we kiss them fondly, we carry them about, we read them again and again, yet there are many thousands of Christians who, although they are learned in other respects, never read, however, the evangelical and apostolic books in an entire lifetime. The Mohammedans hold fast to their doctrines, the Jews also today from the very cradle study the books of Moses. Why do not we in the same way distinguish ourselves in Christ? Those who profess the way of life of Benedict hold, study, absorb a rule written by man, and by one nearly uneducated for the uneducated. Those who are in the Augustinian order are well versed in the rule of their founder. The Franciscans reverence and love the little traditions of their Francis, and to whatever corner of the earth they go, they carry them with them; they do not feel safe unless the little book is on their person. Why do these men attribute more to a rule written by man than does the Christian world to its rule, which Christ delivered to all and which all have equally professed in baptism? Finally, although you may even cite a thousand rules, can anything be holier than this? And I wish that this may come to pass: just as Paul wrote that the law of Moses was not full of glory compared with the glory of the Gospel succeeding it, so may all Christians hold the Gospels and Letters of the Apostles as so holy that in comparison with them these other writings do not seem holy. What others may wish to concede to Albert the Great, to Alexander, to Thomas, to Egidio, to Richard, to Occam, they will certainly be free, as far as I am concerned, to do, for I do not want to diminish the fame of anyone or contend with the studies of men that are now of long standing.[4] However learned these may be, however subtle, however seraphic, if they like, yet they must admit that the former are the most tried and true. Paul wishes that the spirits of those prophesying be judged whether they are of God. Augustine, reading every kind of book with discretion, asks nothing more than a just hearing also for his own works. But in this literature alone [i.e. Holy Scripture] what I do not comprehend, I nevertheless revere. It is no school of

[4] The names are those of medieval theologians: Albert the Great, Alexander of Hales, Thomas Aquinas, Egidio of Rome, Richard of St. Victor, and William of Occam.

theologians who has attested to this Author for us but the
Heavenly Father Himself through the testimony of the
divine voice, and He has done this on two occasions: first at
the Jordan at the time of the Baptism, then on Mount
Tabor at the Transfiguration. "This is my beloved Son,"
He says, "in whom I am well pleased; hear Him."[5] O solid
and truly irrefragable authority, as the theologians say!
What is this phrase, "Hear Him"? Certainly He is the one
and only teacher, let us be the disciples of Him alone. Let
each one extol in his studies his own author as much as he
will wish, this utterance has been said without exception of
Christ alone. A dove first descended on Him, the confirma-
tion of the Father's testimony. Peter next bears His spirit,
to whom the highest Pastor three times entrusted the feeding of His sheep, feeding them without a doubt, however,
on the food of Christian doctrine.[6] This spirit was born
again, as it were, in Paul, whom He himself called a "chosen
vessel" and an extraordinary herald of His name.[7] What
John had drawn from that sacred font of His heart, he expressed in his own writings. What, I pray, is like this in
Scotus (I do not wish that this remark be taken as a pretext
for abuse), what is like this in Thomas? Nevertheless, I
admire the talents of the one, and I also revere the sanctity
of the other. But why do not all of us apply ourselves to
philosophy in these authors of such great value? Why do we
not carry them about on our persons, have them ever in our
hands? Why do we not hunt through these authors, thoroughly examine them, assiduously investigate them? Why
devote the greater part of life to Averroës rather than to
the Gospels? Why spend nearly all of life on the ordinances
of men and on opinions in contradiction with themselves?
The latter, in fact, may now be the views of the more emi-

5 Matthew 3:17; 17:5.
6 John 21:15 ff.
7 Acts 9:15.

nent theologians, if you please; but certainly the first steps of the great theologian in the days to come will be in these authors [of Holy Scripture].

Let all those of us who have pledged in baptism in the words prescribed by Christ, if we have pledged sincerely, be directly imbued with the teachings of Christ in the midst of the very embraces of parents and the caresses of nurses. For that which the new earthen pot of the soul first imbibes settles most deeply and clings most tenaciously. Let the first lispings utter Christ, let earliest childhood be formed by the Gospels of Him whom I would wish particularly presented in such a way that children also might love Him. For as the severity of some teachers causes children to hate literature before they come to know it, so there are those who make the philosophy of Christ sad and morose, although nothing is more sweet than it. In these studies, then, let them engage themselves until at length in silent growth they mature into strong manhood in Christ. The literature of others is such that many have greatly repented the effort expended upon it, and it happens again and again that those who have fought through all their life up to death to defend the principles of that literature, free themselves from the faction of their author at the very hour of death. But happy is that man whom death takes as he meditates upon this literature [of Christ]. Let us all, therefore, with our whole heart covet this literature, let us embrace it, let us continually occupy ourselves with it, let us fondly kiss it, at length let us die in its embrace, let us be transformed in it, since indeed studies are transmuted into morals. As for him who cannot pursue this course (but who cannot do it, if only he wishes?), let him at least reverence this literature enveloping, as it were, His divine heart. If anyone shows us the footprints of Christ, in what manner, as Christians, do we prostrate ourselves, how we adore them! But why do we not venerate instead the living and breathing likeness of Him in these books? If anyone displays the tunic of Christ, to what corner of the earth shall we not hasten so that we may kiss it? Yet were you to bring forth His entire wardrobe, it would not manifest Christ more clearly and truly than the Gospel writings. We embellish a wooden or stone statue with gems and gold for the love of Christ. Why not, rather, mark with gold and gems and with ornaments of greater value than these, if such there be, these writings which bring Christ to us so much more effectively than any paltry image? The latter represents only the form of the body—if indeed it represents anything of Him—but these writings bring you the living image of His holy mind and the speaking, healing, dying, rising Christ himself, and thus they render Him so fully present that you would see less if you gazed upon Him with your very eyes.

V

Letter to Paul Volz

AUGUST 14, 1518

This letter was written as the preface to the new edition of the *Enchiridion militis christiani* which Froben published in the summer of 1518.[1] It is addressed to Paul Volz, abbot of the Benedictine monastery of Hugshofen, near Schlettstadt (Sélestat) in Alsace, a man whose life Erasmus considered an example of the precepts which he himself set down in the *Enchiridion*. Volz (1480–1544) had become a Benedictine in 1503 and had been elected abbot of Hugshofen in 1512, at which time he undertook the reform of his monastic community. He was also associated with the literary circle of Schlettstadt, which included such humanists as Beatus Rhenanus and James Wimpfeling. By 1526 he had gone over to Protestantism, though as "an Erasmian who had strayed into Lutheranism" he had some difficulties in the Lutheran fold.[2] He remained always on good terms with Erasmus, and Erasmus left him a small sum in his will.

The letter is an important statement of Erasmus' basic themes and has been called "a veritable Erasmian manifesto of the religion of pure spirit."[3] Both the scholastic theologians and the monks come in for some harsh criticism because of their departure from the pure and simple "philosophy of Christ." It contains many interesting features:

[1] The Latin text is in Allen, III, 361–77. The only previous English version appears to be one attributed to William Tyndale and published in London in 1533 along with the *Enchiridion*. Erasmus, *A Book called in Latin Enchiridion Militis Christiani and in English The Manual of the Christian Knight* (London, 1905) is a modern replica edition of this earlier work. The present translation was made by the editor from Allen with reference to the Tyndale text.

[2] Roland Crahay and Marie Delcourt (eds.), *Douze Lettres d'Erasme* (Paris, 1938), p. 76. See also Allen, II, 159.

[3] A. Renaudet, *Etudes érasmiennes* (Paris, 1939), p. 175.

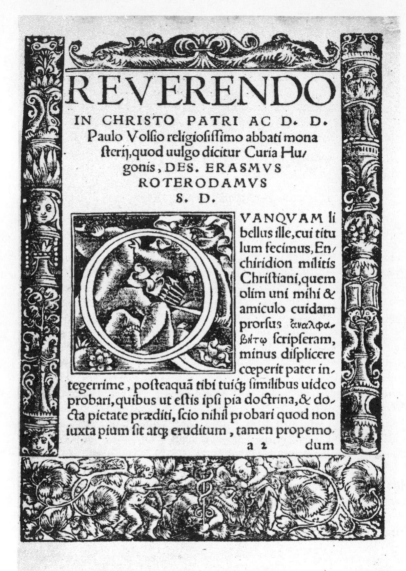

REVERENDO

IN CHRISTO PATRI AC D. D.
Paulo Volfio religiofiſſimo abbati mona
ſterij, quod uulgo dicitur Curia Hu,
gonis, DES. ERASMVS
ROTERODAMVS
S. D.

VANQVAM li
bellus ille, cui titu
lum fecimus, En,
chiridion militis
Chriſtiani, quem
olim uni mihi &
amiculo cuidam
prorſus ἀναλφα,
βήτῳ ſcripſeram,
minus diſplicere
cœperit pater in,
tegerrime, poſteaquã tibi tuiſcɟ ſimilibus uidco
probari, quibus ut eſtis ipſi pia doctrina, & do,
cta pietate præditi, ſcio nihil probari quod non
iuxta pium ſit atcɟ eruditum, tamen propemo,
a 2   dum

First page of Erasmus' letter to Paul Volz in Froben's 1519
edition of the *Enchiridion militis Christiani*. Courtesy of the Rare
Book Division of the New York Public Library.

an emphasis on the conversion of the Turks rather than war against them, for which purpose a commission of pious and learned men would draw up a concise statement of Christian doctrine; a fairly obvious reference to Luther's Ninety-five Theses; and, in the version here presented, a significant addition, which Erasmus inserted in 1529, explaining the laudable purpose and character of early monasticism.

The letter was translated into German in 1520 by Luther's close friend Spalatin and was published the following year. An English translation, prefacing the *Enchiridion* in English, appeared in 1533 and is attributed to William Tyndale. The *Enchiridion* itself was originally written in 1501 and was published for the first time at Antwerp in 1503.

TO THE REVEREND FATHER IN CHRIST, PAUL VOLZ, MOST DEVOUT ABBOT OF THE MONASTERY OF HUGSHOFEN, GREETINGS FROM DESIDERIUS ERASMUS OF ROTTERDAM:

Although that little book entitled *Enchiridion militis christiani,* which I had once written for myself alone and for an untutored friend, began to be less displeasing, most virtuous father, after I learned that it was approved by you and by others like you—who, endowed as you yourselves are with pious learning and with learned piety, would certainly not approve anything that is not pious as well as learned—it nevertheless begins now almost to please when I see that even though it has often been printed, it is ever in demand as if it were a new work, unless the printers are completely deceiving me. Yet that remark repeatedly troubles my mind which a certain learned friend once expressed very wittily (he was joking, but I wish that there were neither truth nor wit in it!): "I see more sanctity in the book than in its author." And this is all the more distressing to me, because the same jest applies to him whose conversion was the chief aim of the work, since indeed this man has not so much torn himself away from the court as immersed himself more deeply in it day by day, with what increase of piety I know not, but I do know to what great disaster, as he himself admits. Nevertheless, I do not entirely grieve for my friend, for, though he has not wished to follow my warnings, some day with misfortune as the teacher he may return to his senses. As for me, though up to now I continue to struggle forward, my guardian spirit assails me with so many mishaps and trials that Homer's Ulysses seems like another Polycrates alongside me.

I do not altogether regret this work, however, if it arouses in so many the desire for true piety. Nor do I think that every kind of reproach should be levelled against me if I fall short of my own counsels. First of all, it is a part of piety to wish truly to become pious; and I do not believe that a heart filled with such intentions should be disdained, even if at times the effort is not crowned with success. One must ever make the effort throughout life, and success on occasion comes to him who has tried again and again. But he has traveled a good part of a difficult journey who has become well acquainted with the way. Therefore I am not moved by the jests of those who scorn this little book as not being learned enough or as one which could be written by any schoolboy, because it does not discuss the questions of the Scotists. As if nothing is learned without these! Let this little book not be sharp-witted provided it be pious. Let it not prepare a person for the mental gymnastics of the Sorbonne but for Christian peace of soul. Let it not contribute to theological argument but to a theological life. What is to be gained by discussing that which everyone discusses? Who today is not occupied with theological questions? With what else are the swarms of schoolmen concerned? There are almost as many commentaries on the *Sentences* as there are theologians. What other kind or category of manual writer is there except those who blend over and again one manual with another and, in the fashion of a pharmacist, repeatedly

concoct the old out of the new, the new out of the old, one
out of many, and many out of one? How could the great
mass of these volumes teach us to live properly when not
even a lifetime is enough to read them? It is as if a doctor
would prescribe to a patient seriously ill that he read the
books of Jacobus a Partibus and all others of a similar character, wherein he will find the remedy to restore his health.
But in the meantime the patient dies, nor will there be anyone who can be helped.

In such a fleeting life it is necessary to have a ready
remedy at hand. In how many volumes do these writers give
instruction about restitution, confession, vows, scandal, and
innumerable other matters? And though they examine
minutely each single topic and so define each as if they mistrusted the abilities of all the other writers, indeed even as
if they mistrusted the goodness of Christ, while they set
forth precisely how He ought to reward or punish each deed,
yet they fail to agree among themselves, nor do they often
explain anything clearly if they are more closely consulted.
There is so great a variety either of abilities or of circumstances. Moreover, even though they define everything truly
and correctly, and aside from the fact that these questions
are treated in a cold and meagre way, how many have the
time to read such volumes? Who can carry around with him
Aquinas' *Secundae secunda*? And yet it is important for all
to live a good life, the path to which Christ intended to be
accessible to all, not by way of a difficult labyrinth of argument but by a sincere faith and by an unfeigned charity
which a confident hope accompanies. Finally, let the great
masters, who of necessity are few in numbers, study these
huge volumes; none the less, the untrained multitude for
whom Christ died must be considered. However, he has
taught the chief part of Christian piety who has enkindled
the love for it. That wise king instructing his son in true

wisdom devotes even more effort to encouraging him than to teaching him, as if to love wisdom is almost to obtain it. What is disgraceful in the case of lawyers and doctors who industriously complicate their art so that at the same time their income may be larger and their prestige among the unskilled may be greater, that would be far more disgraceful to do in the case of the philosophy of Christ. Rather we must strive to render this art as simple as possible and accessible to all. Let our aim be not to appear learned but to lead as many as possible to a Christian life.

War is now being prepared against the Turks, and regardless of the plan behind it we must pray that it be turned not to the advantage of a certain few but to the common good of all. But what do we think would happen if we set before the vanquished (for I don't believe that we shall put them all to the sword), in order to win them to Christ, the works of Occam or Durandus or Scotus or Gabriel or Alvarus? What will they think, what impression will they get (for they are certainly men, if nothing else) when they hear those thorny and intricate arguments about instances, formalities, quiddities, and relationships? Especially when they see those great professors of religion disagreeing about these matters among themselves to the point that they frequently grow pale and insult and spit at one another and sometimes even exchange blows, or when they see the Dominicans contending at close hand and afar in behalf of their Thomas, and the Franciscans guarding with joined shields their most subtle and seraphic doctors, some speaking as nominalists, others as realists. What, indeed, will they think if they see that the question is so difficult that it has never adequately been settled what words should be used in speaking of Christ? As though one is dealing with some wayward spirit who is evoked to your own destruction if prescribed words are not carefully followed and not, instead, with the most merciful Saviour, who demands only that we live a pure and simple life. I implore you by the everlasting God, what will happen in this state of affairs, especially if our morals and our life correspond to this arrogant teaching? If the Turks should observe our ambition because of our loud, tyrannical clamoring, our avarice because of our plundering, our lust because of our debauchery, our cruelty because of our oppressive rule, how shall we press upon them the doctrine of Christ, so contrary to all these things? The most efficacious way of overcoming the Turks would be if they beheld that which Christ taught and exemplified shining forth in our own lives, if they perceived that we do not covet their empires nor thirst after their gold nor seek their possessions, but strive for nothing except their salvation and Christ's glory. This is that true, authentic, and efficacious theology which in times gone by subdued for Christ both the pride of the philosophers and the unconquered scepters of the princes. And if we act thus, Christ himself will be with us.

And indeed it is not fitting that we proclaim ourselves good Christians with this argument if we kill as many as possible, but rather if we save as many as possible; not if we sacrifice many thousands of infidels to Hell, but if we render faithful as many of the infidels as possible; not if we curse them with dire execrations, but if we desire and devoutly pray that Heaven grant them deliverance and a better attitude of mind. And if this be not our disposition, it will sooner come to pass that we shall degenerate into Turks rather than win the Turks to our side. And although the dice of war, ever uncertain, fall favorably, it will happen that the pope or his cardinals perhaps may rule more widely, but not Christ, whose kingdom flourishes at last only if piety, charity, peace, and chastity thrive. This rule we trust shall be under the leadership and guidance of the excellent Leo X, unless he is diverted from his endeavors for what is best into another direction by the surge of human affairs. Christ himself declares that He is the protector and prince of the heavenly kingdom, which has a splendor only if what is heavenly is triumphant.

For Christ certainly did not die so that the might, the wealth, the arms, and the rest of the pomp of a worldly kingdom, which once were in the hands of the pagans, or at least of secular princes not so very different from the pagans, be now turned over to some priests. In my opinion we should seriously consider influencing their minds with letters and tracts long before we resort to arms. But with what kind of letters? Not with threatening letters, not with tyrannical letters, but with letters which truly breathe a paternal charity, which echo the heart of Peter and Paul, and which not only bear an apostolic inscription but have the flavor of apostolic power. I say this not because I do not know that the whole font and course of Christian philosophy is concealed in the Gospels and Epistles, but because the strange and frequently involved language as well as the figures of speech and oblique metaphors give such difficulty that even we ourselves must often make a great effort before we understand them. Thus, in my opinion, it would be most convenient if the task were assigned to some men as pious as they are learned to draw together in a short statement the whole philosophy of Christ from the most pure sources of the Gospels and the Epistles and from the most approved interpreters, and to do this with simplicity in so far as it is still learned and with brevity in so far as it is still clear. Let those things which pertain to faith be related in as few propositions as possible. Let those things which pertain to the way of life be communicated also in a few statements, and let them be transmitted in such a way that they [the recipients] may understand that the yoke of Christ is sweet and agreeable, not harsh, that they have found fathers, not tyrants, shepherds, not robbers, and that they are called to salvation, not dragged away into slavery. They also are men, nor are their hearts of iron or steel. They can be softened, they can be won over by friendly acts, whereby even wild beasts are tamed. And especially efficacious is Christian truth. But the Roman pontiff shall order at the same time those to whom he wishes to assign this work not to depart in any way from the model of Christ nor anywhere to show regard for the desires and passions of men.

It was such a book that I had in mind to produce at the time when I pounded out the *Enchiridion*. I saw that the mass of Christians had been corrupted not only in their feelings but also in their opinions. I carefully considered that very many of those who profess to be shepherds and teachers abused the titles of Christ for their own advantage, to say nothing whatsoever in the meanwhile about those at whose command and prohibition human affairs are sent scurrying in all directions, and at whose vices, although they are public, one is scarcely permitted to groan. And in such great darkness, amid such worldly confusion, in the face of so great a variety of human opinions, where should we have recourse rather than to the truly sacred anchor of the Gospel teaching? Who, truly pious, does not see and lament over this age, the most corrupt by far? When did tyranny, when did avarice ever hold sway more widely or with more impunity? When was more attention ever paid to ceremonies? When has injustice abounded more freely? When has charity grown so cold? What is asserted, what is read, what is heard, what is proposed except that which savors of ambition and greed? Oh, how unhappy we would be if Christ had not left us some sparks of His teaching and living and the everlasting veins, as it were, of His own mind. Therefore we must strive in this direction so that, after we have set aside the coals of men, we may stir up these sparks—I willingly use the Pauline word—and we may explore these veins until we find the living water flowing to eternal life. We delve deep down into our earth in order to mine that which nourishes our vices. Are we not, then, to turn over the richest earth of Christ in order to obtain the salvation of souls? No cold blast of vice ever so extinguished the flame of charity that it could not be restored from this flintstone. The stone is Christ, but this stone is a seedbed of heavenly fire and has veins of living water. Abraham in times past dug wells in all the land, seeking everywhere veins of living water. But these same wells, having been filled up with earth by the Philistines, were reopened by Isaac and his servants; and not content with restoring the former wells, he also dug new ones. Once again the Philistines incite quarrels and strife, yet he does not stop his digging.

And in these times Philistines are not entirely lacking to whom the earth is more pleasing than the lively bubbling of springs; indeed, those who have a taste for earthly things and turn aside to earthly desires, force the teaching of the Gospel, which they make a servant to human ambition, into compliance with base profit and their own tyranny. And if any Isaac or anyone from his family should dig and discover some pure vein, immediately they raise a clamor and cry out against him, well aware that this vein would check their profit and hinder their ambition, although it served the glory of Christ. Then they throw earth in and stop up the vein with a corrupt interpretation and drive away the digger, or at least they so defile the water with mud and filth that he who drinks it henceforth imbibes more slime and dirt than pure liquid. They do not wish that they who thirst after justice should drink of pure liquid, but they lead them to their own worn-out cisterns which contain rubble but not water. Nevertheless, the real children of Isaac, the true worshipers of Christ, must not be wearied by this labor. For those men who cast earth onto the wellsprings of the Gospel also wish to be considered among the worshipers of Christ, so that among Christians now it is not at all safe to teach Christ purely. So great has the strength of the Philistines become, waging war in behalf of the earth, preaching earthly things in place of what is heavenly, human precepts in place of the divine, that is to say, preaching not what serves Christ's glory but what is to the profit of those who trade in indulgences, agreements, dispensations, and similar bargains. And they do this with greater danger because they cloak their cupidity with the titles of great princes, of the supreme pontiff, and even of Christ himself. But yet no one more truly carries out the task of the pope than he who teaches purely the heavenly philosophy of Christ, of which the pope is the first teacher. No one deserves better of princes than he who labors that the commonweal may flourish as greatly as possible and may be burdened with the least possible oppression.

But here someone from the army of the schools will shout: "It is easy for anyone to prescribe in general what is to be followed and what is to be avoided; but in the meantime what will the response be to those who seek advice on so many specific matters and particular cases?" First, there are too many kinds of human affairs to permit a sure response to each one of them. Secondly, so great is the variety of circumstances that unless they are known, one cannot even give a certain reply. Finally, I do not know if these men have a sure answer to give, especially since they disagree about most things among themselves. And those who are the more sensible in this contingent are not accustomed to reply thus: "You shall do this, you shall avoid that"; but rather: "In my opinion this is the safer course, this I think is tolerable." But if we have that simple and clear eye of the Gospel, if the house of our soul has the lamp of pure faith set on the lampstand, those petty matters will easily be dispersed as if they were shadows. If the rule of Christian charity is at hand, everything else will easily conform to it. But what must you do when this rule will clash with those practices which have been accepted in the public usage of the ages and which have been sanctioned by the laws of princes? For this frequently occurs. You may not condemn what princes do in the fulfillment of their duty. But on the other hand, do not corrupt the heavenly philosophy of Christ with human decrees. Let Christ remain that which He is, the center with a number of circles surrounding Him. Do not move the target from its own central position. Those who are nearest to Christ, priests, bishops, cardinals, popes, and all whose duty it is to follow the Lamb wheresoever He shall go, let them embrace what is most pure, and as far as they can, let them transfer this to those nearest to them. The second circle comprises secular princes, whose arms and whose laws serve Christ in their own fashion, either while in just war they overcome the enemy and defend the public peace, or while with lawful punishment they restrain evildoers. And yet because they are of necessity engaged in those affairs which are connected with the lowest dregs of the earth and with the business of the world, there is the danger that they might slip farther from the center, that they might wage war not for the commonweal but for their own pleasure, that under the pretext of justice they might vent their fury even on those whom clemency could restore, that under the title of lord they might plunder the people whose property they had the duty to protect.

Moreover, as Christ like a fountain of everlasting fire draws next to Him the order of priests and makes them fiery and purifies them from all earthly stain, so it is the duty of priests, and especially of the highest priests, to call princes to their side, as far as they may. If war should break out anywhere, let the popes strive for a settlement of the issues without bloodshed, or, if that is impossible, since there are tempests in human affairs, at least let them do their best that war be waged with less bloodshed and not be drawn out for a long time. In former times the bishops' authority intervened even in cases of just penalties and repeatedly wrested the guilty one from the hands of the judges, as Augustine openly bears witness in his letters. For certain things are so necessary to the order of the commonwealth that Christ nevertheless has ignored them in part, in part has rejected them, and in part has neither disapproved nor approved, as if He closed His eyes at them. He does not recognize the coin of Caesar nor the inscription on it. Thus it is that He orders tribute to be paid if it is due, as if it is of little concern to Him, provided that that which is due to God is given Him. He neither condemns nor openly absolves the adulterous woman, but He bids her not to repeat her crime. Concerning those condemned by Pilate, whose blood he had mixed with their sacrifices, He does not pronounce whether they suffered this rightly or wrongly, but He threatens a like destruction for all unless they return to their senses. Moreover, when He was asked to settle the division of an inheritance, He openly refused the task, as if to judge such crass issues was unworthy of Him who taught heavenly things. On the other hand, there are things which He openly abominates. He thunders "Woe!" against the greedy Pharisees, the hypocrites, the exalted rich. He never rebukes the Apostles more sharply than when they are moved by the desire for revenge or the stirrings of ambition. To those asking if they should bid fire come down from heaven to consume the city which had shut them out, He says, "You know not of what spirit you are." When Peter attempts to call Him away from the cross and back to the world, He calls him Satan. In how many ways and how often does He recall those disputing over first rank to a different frame of mind! Also there is that which He explicitly teaches and prescribes: not to resist evil, to deserve well of enemies, to be gentle of soul, and other precepts of the same character.

These injunctions must be sorted out and each must be arranged in its proper place. Let us not therefore immediately make Christ the author of that which is done by princes or secular officials, nor claim that it is done by divine right, as they now say. Certain gross matters are dealt with by these men, not entirely possessing a Christian purity but which nevertheless must not be reproached, inasmuch as they are necessary for the maintenance of order. For by the service of these men we are not made good, but less evil, and those who are evil do less harm to the commonwealth. Therefore their honor is due to them, since they do in some manner serve divine justice and the public peace, without which the work of piety is sometimes thrown into confusion. They should be honored when they perform their duty, they should perhaps be endured when they exercise their power in their own interests, lest a greater evil arise. For the image, or rather the shadow, of divine justice gleams in them also, which however ought to shine forth with far greater sharpness, clarity, and purity in the morals and laws of priests. An image is reflected in one way in iron, in another way in a mirror of glass.

In the third circle let us place the common people, as the grossest part of this world, but gross as it is still belonging to the body of Christ. For not only are the eyes members of the body but also the legs, feet, and the less honorable parts. Thus forbearance must be shown them so that they may always be called, as far as it can be done, to that which is more approved by Christ. For in the body of Christ he who was at one time the foot can become the eye. And as princes, if they are reprobate, should not be embittered by loud reproaches lest, according to the opinion of Augustine, provoked, they stir up more serious tragedies, so the weak people, after the example of Christ who endured and supported his disciples with such gentleness, should be endured and supported with fatherly indulgence until little by little they grow strong in Christ. For piety also has its infancy, its adolescence, its time of full and vigorous strength. Yet all must strive toward Christ, each according to his own strength. Each of the elements has its own place. Fire, however, which occupies the highest place, little by little draws all the others to it and, as far as it can, transforms them into its own nature. It turns clear water into air, the thin air it transforms into itself. Paul made many allowances for the Corinthians, distinguishing meanwhile between what he set forth in the name of the Lord to those who were perfect and what he permitted in his own name to those who were weak; yet he had this hope, that they may make progress. Again, he was anxious over the Galatians until Christ be formed in them.

Now there will be no great contention with the man who will think that this circle ought to be assigned rather to the princes. And indeed, if we are appraising morals, you will scarcely see other Christians more gross; I am speaking of the majority, not of all. But whatever is beyond the third circle, that should be always and everywhere abhorred. This category includes ambition, greed, lust, anger, vengeance, envy, slander, and the other vices, which then indeed become irremediable when, made attractive in the guise of piety and duty, they creep into the higher circles; that is, when under the pretext of justice and the law we behave as a tyrant, when through an opportunity afforded by religion we look to our gain, when under the pretence of defending the Church we strive for worldly power, when that is commanded as if serving the cause of Christ which is farthest from the teaching of Christ. Accordingly everyone must be given a target toward which he must strive. But there is only one target, namely, Christ and his most pure teaching. Therefore if you set forth a worldly target in place of the heavenly one, that man who strives to advance will not have the goal for which he may rightly make the effort. That which is highest must be fixed upon by all of us so that we may at least attain that which is mediocre.

Nor should we banish any kind of life from this target.

The perfection of Christ is in the dispositions, not in the mode of life; in the soul, not in what a person wears or eats. There are among the monks those who are hardly admitted into the outermost circle; and yet I speak of those who are good but weak. There are among the twice married those whom Christ considers worthy of the first circle. Nor, in fact, is injury done in the meantime to any profession of life if what is best and most perfect is set forth before all. Unless by chance it is thought that Plato had insulted all cities because in his *Republic* he set forth the model of such a commonwealth as could not hitherto be seen, or that Quintilian offended the whole class of orators because he invented such a model orator as thus far did not exist. Are you far distant from the archetype? You should not give up but should encourage yourself to go forward. You are not far off? You should urge yourself to come nearer. For no one has advanced so far that he does not have farther to go.

Every kind of life, however, has certain perils connected with it which cause a degeneration. He who clearly points out these dangers does not detract from an order but acts in its interest. The happiness of princes, for instance, is exposed to tyranny and a prey to folly, flattery, and pleasure. The man who shows what must be avoided deserves well of the order of princes. Nor does he diminish the majesty of these princes, in which they glory, who explains on what the true majesty of princes depends, who reminds them of what they swore when they undertook their princely office and of what their obligations are to their people and to their magistrates. Ecclesiastical princes have a near affinity with two vices above all, avarice and ambition. As if perceiving this beforehand, that first shepherd after Christ warns the bishops to feed their flocks, not to rob or flay them; and not to feed them for the sake of base gain but out of a free and ready will, nor to lord it over them, but to rouse them to piety by the examples of their lives rather than by threats or commands. Will he then be seen to detract from the priestly order who reminds them by what means bishops are truly great, powerful, and rich? Moreover, the class of monks is practically the companion, besides other vices, of superstition, pride, hypocrisy, and disparagement. He then does not forthwith condemn their way of life who warns wherein true religion is located, and how far distant truly Christian piety is from pride and genuine charity from deceit, and how venomous language is at odds with pure religion, especially if he shows what should be avoided in such a gentle way that no man is marked out nor any class attacked. What, however, in the course of human affairs is so fortunate that it has no vices accompanying it? Therefore, just as he aids, not injures, the health of the body whosoever makes known what is harmful or beneficial to true health, so he does not draw men away from religion but rather exhorts them to it, who shows how true religion can be corrupted and restored.

For I hear that certain men so interpret the precepts of this little book as if they estrange men's minds from the monastic life, because less is attributed to ceremonies than certain men who attribute far too much wish, nor also is much conceded to human ordinances. And what is more, nothing can be said so cautiously that the wicked do not turn it into some false accusation or into an occasion for sin, with the result that now it is hardly safe to give any suitable advice. If anyone should deter men from the wars which, more than the pagans ever did, we have been waging now for some time and for objectives of no importance, he is marked out by the tricksters as if he holds with those who deny that Christians should wage any war. For we have made heretics out of the authors of this opinion because some pope seems to approve of war. He is not censured, however, who, contrary to the teaching of Christ and the Apostles, blows the trumpet to summon men to war for any and every cause. If anyone recalls that it is truly apostolic to draw the Turks to religion with the help of Christ rather than by arms, he is immediately suspected of teaching, as it were, that the Turks should in no way be checked if they attack Christians. If anyone praises the simplicity of the Apostles and comments on the extravagance of these times, there are those who reprimand him as favoring the Ebionites. If anyone more emphatically urges that those who are married should be joined together more by piety and the agreement of their minds than by the embrace of their bodies and that they should live their married life so purely that it resembles virginity as closely as possible, he comes under suspicion of holding with the Marcionites the idea that all sexual intercourse is impure. If anyone warns that disputations, particularly theological ones, should be free from a vain pertinacity in having one's own way and in maintaining one's own opinions and free also from that theatrical ambition to display one's strength, he is improperly arraigned as if he condemned all the schools. For Saint Augustine, when he warns the dialecticians to be on their guard against a love of quarreling, does not condemn dialectics but exposes a vice connected with it, so that it might be avoided.

Likewise, if anyone reproaches the perverse judgment of the crowd, which assigns first place among the virtues to those in the lowest class and, on the other side, detests most furiously those vices which are the least wicked when there are far more terrible ones, and vice versa, immediately he is hailed into court as if he is in favor of those vices before which he places a more serious vice or as if he damns those good deeds to which he prefers others as more holy. For instance, if anyone warns that it is safer to trust in good deeds than in papal pardons, he certainly does not condemn these pardons but gives preference to that which is of greater certainty according to Christ's teaching. Likewise, if anyone admonishes that those do better who work hard at

home to support their wife and children than if they go off
to see Rome, Jerusalem, or Compostella and that the money
spent on a long and perilous journey is more devoutly given
to the good and deserving poor, he does not condemn the
pious disposition of such pilgrims but prefers that which is
closer to true piety.[4]

Now indeed it is not only in our times that certain vices
are detested just as if they were the only vices, while we
treat others lightly as if they were not vices, although they
may be more terrible than the ones we so execrate. Augustine
complains in his letters that among the Africans the one
charge of lust is imputed as a vice to priests, whereas avarice
and drunkenness are construed almost as praise. We magnify this one vice in tragic style, viewing it again and again
as a dreadful crime for the same hands to touch the body of
Christ which have touched the body of a prostitute. Nor
are they lacking who, too much in the manner of a tragedy,
have dared to assert publicly that it is a lesser fault for a
woman to have intercourse with a brute beast than with a
priest. The man who rebukes these shameless statements
does not necessarily approve of incontinent priests, but he
warns that those vices are disregarded which should have
been given greater attention. The priest is a gambler, an old
war horse or public brawler, an ignoramus, one completely
immersed in worldly affairs, one devoted to the evil service
of evil princes, yet they do not cry out in like manner against
him who totally worldly performs the sacred mysteries. The
priest is a deceiver who with his poison tongue and his fabricated lies ruins the reputation of an innocent man who has
even deserved well, why then at this point do we not cry out,
"Oh, shocking crime! With your tongue stained with the
poison of hell, with your mouth whereby you slay an inno-

---

[4] The above two sentences would seem to refer to Luther's warnings about
papal pardons in his Ninety-five Theses, specifically to Theses 41 to 46. These
were now in wide circulation and the great controversy inaugurated by them
had begun.

cent man, you take unto yourself and consume the body of Him who has died even for the reprobate"? But we so disregard this evil that those who profess the most strict religious observances almost take praise from it. They deserve to be reprehended who openly maintain concubines at home and give thereby a dangerous example to the people. Who denies it? But this other vice is much more hateful to Christ. He who prefers honey does not therefore disapprove of butter; nor does he recommend fever who warns that madness is more to be avoided. And it is not easy to say how great a corruption of morals springs from perverse judgments of this kind.

Certain things have now been received into the rank of the virtues in such a way that they have the mask rather than the essence of piety, to the extent that, unless you take care, they utterly extinguish true piety. If there were concealed the blight of an indifferent religion in ceremonies, Paul in all his Epistles would not have become so violently angry at these. Nevertheless, in any case we do not condemn ceremonies moderately observed, but we do not allow that in these we have the beginning and end of sanctity, as they say. Saint Augustine even forbade the clergy whom he maintained at home to wear striking attire; and [his attitude was that] if they wished to find favor with the people, let them find favor by their morals, not their dress. Nowadays how much new and wonderful raiment there is! However, I do not inveigh against that; this I wonder at, that too much is attributed to those things which perhaps by right could be reprehended, and on the other hand so little to those things which alone should receive attention. I do not reproach the Franciscans or Benedictines because they prize their own rule but because certain of these men ascribe more to their own rules than to the Gospel. Would that this charge did not apply to most of them! I do not belabor the point that some live on fish, others on beans and herbs, others on eggs, but I warn emphatically that they err who in a Judaic spirit put on the conviction of justice because of this and who, because of this kind of nonsense invented by little men, place themselves before others, while they do not consider it a vice to assail another's reputation with their lies. Christ nowhere prescribes anything about the choice of food, nor do the Apostles, but Paul often advises to the contrary. Christ abhors poisonous defamation, the Apostolic Epistles abominate it. And yet in the former case we wish to appear scrupulous, and in the latter we are brave and intrepid. Does he, I beg, seem to harm religion who gives these admonitions not only in a general way but also with love? However, who is so foolish that he wishes to be considered eloquent for bringing to light the vices of monks? But these men are afraid that they will have fewer listeners and then that fewer people will present themselves for admission into their flock. Yet no one is more obedient and subject to authority, to use the Pauline expression, than he who, after he has drunk in the spirit of Christ, begins to be free. True charity takes account of everything good, endures everything, refuses nothing, is obedient to those in authority, not only to those who are benign and agreeable but even to those who are harsh and surly.

But yet those in power must in the meantime be on guard lest they turn another's obedience into their own tyranny and lest, on that account, they prefer men who are superstitious rather than pious because they may be more obedient to every nod. They delight in being called fathers. But what father in the flesh desires his children always to be infants so that he may have more control over them for his own pleasure? On the other hand, those who make progress toward the liberty of Christ should take care in the beginning lest they make liberty a pretext for sensuality, as Paul warns, or lest they make liberty a cloak for malice, according to Peter's teaching. But if one or another has abused this liberty, it is not necessarily right that everyone be kept in a perpetual Judaism because of this. Whoever is observant will discover that no one among such persons draws more tightly the snares of ceremonies than those who hold sway under this pretense and live by their belly, not by Christ.

Yet in fact, it is not that they fear that the race of Essenes might not be propagated among so great a variety of temperaments and spirits, in as much as it happens that there is indeed nothing anywhere so absurd that many do not seek after it. Nevertheless, these men ought to be more desirous of having sincere and true professors of religion than of having many. And would that the law provided that no one might be entangled in snares of this kind before his thirtieth year, before he himself came to know himself or the power of true religion was known! On the other hand, those who conduct their business like the Pharisees, traveling over land and sea to make one convert, nowhere fail to find inexperienced youths whom they inveigle into their net and take prisoner. There is a vast number of fools and simple people everyplace. I should certainly desire, nor do I doubt that everyone truly pious desires the same, that the religion of the Gospel so penetrate the hearts of all that no one, satisfied with it, may seek a Benedictine or Franciscan religion; nor do I doubt that Benedict himself or Francis desires the same. Moses applauds when obscured by the glory of Christ; they also should applaud if, for love of the law of the Gospel, human constitutions are of small account to us. I should wish that all Christians live in such a way that those who alone are now called religious appear not religious enough. And today this is true in many cases; why conceal obvious facts? And yet in former times the first origin of the monastic life was a withdrawal from the barbarism of the idolaters. The rules of the monks following soon after this were nothing else than a calling back to

Christ. The courts of princes were at one time more Christian in title than in life. Then the disease of ambition and avarice laid hold of the bishops. The people likewise lost the warmth of that primitive charity. Hence Benedict earnestly sought a retreat, and after him Bernard, and then one and another. These chosen few agreed in nothing else than in a pure and simple Christianity.

But if anyone examines more attentively the life and rules of Benedict, Francis, or Augustine, he will observe that what they wished was only to live with willing friends in liberty of spirit close to the Gospel teaching; and that they had been forced to prescribe to some extent about clothing and food and other outward matters, undoubtedly fearful lest more be attributed, as is often the case, to the human ordinances of men than to the Gospel. They dreaded wealth, they fled honors, even ecclesiastical ones. They labored with their hands not only that they themselves might not be a burden to anyone but that there might be an abundance from which to help others in need. They occupied mountain peaks, they nested in marshy places, they dwelt in sandy and abandoned regions. At length they tamed a great multitude of men without reproaches, scourgings, and prisons but by teaching alone, by counsel, by service, and by the example of their lives. Such were the monks whom Basil loves and praises, whom Chrysostom defends; there was complete agreement among these men, as Saint Jerome writes to Marcella, that the troop of monks and virgins is the flower and the most precious jewel among the ornaments of the Church. It is wonderful to relate how today monks of every kind flatter themselves with this statement. But we shall allow them to embrace the praise if at the same time they embrace the example. Moreover, the most prudent man suggests this image of the monks whom he has judged worthy of that title: "A dissonant voice indeed," he says, "but one religion. Almost as many choruses of psalm singers as different kinds of people. Meanwhile, and this is certainly the very first virtue among Christians, they arrogate nothing to themselves because of the control of their pride. All strive for humility. Whoever shall have been last, this man is considered first. In their dress there is no distinction, no admiration. It is the cause neither of blame nor of praise however one has been pleased to conduct himself. Fasts also exalt no one, nor is deference paid to total abstinence, nor is a moderate satiety condemned. Each one stands or falls in the sight of his Lord. No one judges another, lest he be judged by the Lord; and what is customary in very many regions, to censure oneself severely, does not entirely prevail here." Thus far this man has painted the picture of the best monks; whoever wishes may compare it with the morals of these times.[5]

Such were the origins of monasticism, such were the patriarchs. Then gradually in the course of time ceremonies increased with riches, genuine piety and simplicity grew cold. And although we see that monasteries everywhere have degenerated to morals that are more than profane, yet the world is burdened with new institutions, as if they also were not going to decline in the same way a short time after. In former times, as I have said, the life of the monks was a withdrawal to solitude. Now they are called monks who are completely occupied in the midst of worldly business, clearly exercising a certain despotic control over human affairs. And yet on account of their attire, on account of some title, they arrogate so much virtue to themselves that in comparison they do not regard others as Christians. Why do we so limit the profession of Christ, which he wished to extend most widely? If we are moved by splendid appellations, I beseech you, what else is a city but a great monastery? Monks are

<hr>

[5] Erasmus added this entire paragraph on early monasticism to the letter when it was published in the Basel *Opus epistolarum* of 1529. It is not found in Tyndale's translation, since he obviously used the earlier edition of the *Enchiridion*.

obedient to their abbot or to those placed in charge; citizens submit to the bishop and their pastors, whom Christ himself, not the authority of men, has set over them. The former live in idleness and are nourished by the generosity of others, possessing in common what has come to them without hard work (I say nothing, meanwhile, about those who are corrupt); the latter, each in proportion to his own wealth, share what they have acquired by their own industry with those in need. Moreover, concerning the vow of chastity, I would not dare to set forth how trifling the difference is between ordinary celibacy and chaste marriage. Finally, we shall not at all miss those three vows devised by men in that person who sincerely and purely has kept first that one and only vow which in baptism we made not to man but to Christ. Now if you compare the bad with the bad from each group, the latter without question are better. But if you compare the good with the good, the difference is very small; if, however, there is any difference, it is only that they seem to be more religious who practice their religion with less coercion. Therefore it remains that one should neither be foolishly pleased with himself on account of a kind of life different from others nor should he despise or condemn another way of life. But in every kind of life let this be the common endeavor of all, that we strive, each according to his own ability, toward that target, which is Christ, set up before us all; and let us exhort and also aid one another toward this goal, neither envying those who hasten on before us in this race nor disdaining the weak who are not yet able to overtake us. At last, when each has done what he could, let him not be like that Pharisee in the Gospel who boasts of his good works before God, "I fast twice a week," etc., but in accordance with Christ's counsel let him say, and let him say from the heart, "I am a useless servant, I have done only what I had to do," and let him say this to himself, not merely to others. No one is more truly trusting than he who is distrustful to this extent. No one is farther from true religion than he who very much seems to himself to be religious. Nor is the situation ever worse with respect to Christian piety than when what is of the world is twisted toward Christ and when the authority of men is preferred to divine authority. We must unite under that one head if we wish to be truly Christian. Moreover, he obeys Christ, not man, who obeys a man calling him to Christ. And he who endures false, cruel, and tyrannical men who teach that which serves not religion but their own domination, he practices Christian patience, provided that what these teachers bid is only injurious and not also unholy. Otherwise it will be fitting to have that Apostolic response at hand: "We must obey God rather than men."

But we have long since exceeded an epistle's length, to such an extent does the time escape our notice when we converse most pleasantly with a most agreeable friend. The book under Froben's imprint, reborn, as it were, and much more polished and free from faults than before, flies to your breast. Certain fragments of our earlier studies have been added. Moreover, it seemed proper that this edition, such as it is, should be linked with you above all, so that he who has taken the precepts of upright living from Erasmus may have an example from Volz immediately at hand. Farewell, good father and outstanding light of the true religion.

Admonish Sapidus[6] with my words that he truly resemble his name, that is, that he continue to be like himself; and Wimpfeling[7] that he make ready his armor, soon to engage the Turks, seeing that he has now waged war long enough with priests who keep concubines. I hope that we shall sometime see him a bishop, conspicuous with his two-horned

---

[6] Sapidus is John Witz, a scholar and teacher at Schlettstadt and a prominent member of the literary circle there.

[7] James Wimpfeling, former rector of the University of Heidelberg, was one of the most distinguished of the German humanists. His last years (1515–1528) were spent at Schlettstadt.

miter and staff, borne aloft on a mule. But, joking aside, in my name extend many greetings both to them and Ruserus[8] and to other friends. Now and then in pure and devout prayers commend the welfare of your Erasmus to the All good and All powerful Christ.

Basel, the Vigil of the Assumption of the Virgin Mother, 1518.

[8] John Ruserus was a priest at Schlettstadt and a former editor for the Schürer press in Strasbourg.

VI

Letter to Albert of Brandenburg

OCTOBER 19, 1519

Albert of Brandenburg (1490–1545) was the young archbishop of Mainz, whose elevation to that important see in 1514 involved large payments to Rome, which in turn occasioned the granting and preaching of the special indulgence that Luther attacked in his Ninety-five Theses. There is therefore a certain irony in Erasmus' addressing this letter, so favorable to Luther, to the man who bore at least some responsibility for the original indulgence controversy. That, of course, was not the point that Erasmus had in mind when he wrote the archbishop. He wished to explain clearly his position with regard to Luther in view of the accusations that now linked him with the Wittenberg reformer, and he desired to alert his distinguished correspondent to the base motives and questionable tactics of those who attacked Luther and himself. The letter is remarkably frank and incisive, considering to whom it was sent, and it is one of the fullest expressions of Erasmus' mind on the Lutheran controversy as it developed through 1519.[1]

Albert himself was an educated man and favorable to the new learning. He had written Erasmus in September 1517 to congratulate him on his edition of the New Testament, and Erasmus had subsequently dedicated his *Ratio verae theologiae,* or *Methodus,* to him. They continued to correspond in 1519. Thus the letter here presented did not arrive entirely out of the blue, and it is particularly interesting to see how Erasmus deftly leads into his subject from his opening words of appreciation for the gold cup Albert had sent him

---

[1] The Latin text is in Allen, IV, 96-107. There is an English translation in R. B. Drummond, *Erasmus: His Life and Character* (London, 1873), II, 33-45. The present translation was made by the editor from Allen.

through their mutual friend Ulrich von Hutten. Erasmus was at the University of Louvain at this time, where once again he had become an object of suspicion and attack because of the growing alarm over Luther.

The letter, though a private one for the archbishop, was soon in wide circulation. Unauthorized versions were published in 1520 in Cologne, Wittenberg, and Nuremberg, and as a result Erasmus included it in a collection of his letters published by Froben in 1521.

To the most reverend Father in Christ, Albert, Cardinal Archbishop, greetings from Erasmus of Rotterdam, theologian:

Many greetings, most reverend Prelate and most illustrious Prince. I received Your Highness's gift, as beautiful and as striking in its material as in its workmanship, and worthy indeed of being sent by such a Prince; but I do not know if its recipient Erasmus, for whom it is more fitting to drink from glass or earthenware than from goblets of gold, is worthy of it. Even if it had been a glass goblet, I would have placed it among my most prized possessions, especially because so distinguished a man had sent it. Moreover, your gift, most welcome in itself, was graciously presented to me by our friend Hutten, who informed me that it is called a cup of love, as if sacred to the Graces, the reason being, I suppose, that when two are joined together by it, as in a kiss, they become one. He added that your cup had the power of binding together in the closest friendship those who drank from it. Wishing to test this, I drank from your cup the health of the most reverend William Cardinal Croy when he visited my study recently, and he in turn drank mine. This youth is a most fortunate young man, and his talents seem worthy of his great good fortune.

But I am sorry that your gift did not arrive sooner. For recently the theologians of Louvain and I made peace, with the understanding that they would restrain the disparaging tongues which they provoke and I, as far as I could, would continue to curb the pens of my friends. At the banquet concluding this arrangement (for nothing is consecrated here without a drinking party) I would have produced your cup, if I had had it, and if each one had drunk from it, perhaps our peace would have been launched under more favorable auspices. For our friendship, never completely restored, has now been disrupted because of a letter of mine which has been misunderstood and badly interpreted, and thus, after a brief calm, the rising storm seems more violent than before.[2] I do not doubt that this is the work of Satan, who hates nothing worse than concord among Christians and on that account tries in every way to disturb somehow or other the tranquillity of life and of learning, and he does this under the pretext of piety in order to do even greater harm.

And so it is that there are a few facts on this subject which it is in my interest that you know, if the pressure of Your Eminence's affairs permits it; and perhaps it is of importance to you as well, as it certainly is to the cause of learning, which, in justice, the best men must support against the worst. In the first place, I must declare that I never had anything to do either with the affair of Reuchlin[3] or with the case of Luther. Cabala and Talmud, whatever they are, never had any appeal to me. Those bitter clashes between Reuchlin and the supporters of Jacob Hochstrat have greatly displeased me. Luther couldn't be more unknown to me, and I have not yet had the time to read his books

[2] The letter Erasmus refers to is a courteous and friendly one he wrote Luther on May 30, 1519. It is translated in Huizinga, op. cit., pp. 229-31. It had evidently just become known at Louvain, probably through Jacob Hochstrat, the Dominican inquisitor at Cologne, who had recently arrived at Louvain to encourage the condemnation of Luther's opinions there. See Etienne, op. cit., pp. 98-99.

[3] The "affair of Reuchlin" refers to the long and bitter quarrel between John Reuchlin, the German scholar and Hebraist, and those who sought his condemnation for heresy because of his defense of the study of Hebrew literature. Hochstrat led the opposition to Reuchlin.

beyond merely sampling a few pages. If he has written well, no praise is due me; if not, I should not be held accountable. I observe this, however, that the best men are the least offended by his writings, not that they approve everything, I suppose, but that they read them in the spirit in which we read Cyprian and Jerome, or rather Peter Lombard, certainly with considerable allowance.

I was sorry that Luther's books were published; and when some or other of his writings first came into view, I made every effort to prevent their publication, chiefly because I feared a disturbance might result from them. Luther had written, in my opinion, a very Christian letter to me, and I replied, advising him in passing not to write anything seditious, nor against the Roman pontiff, nor too arrogantly and passionately, but rather to preach the Gospel teaching in a sincere spirit and with all gentleness. I did this politely, so to accomplish more. I added that there were some here who favored him, with the hope that he might adapt himself more readily to their judgment. Certain simpletons have interpreted this to mean that I favor Luther. Since none of these men have admonished Luther up to now, I alone have admonished him. I am neither Luther's accuser nor his defender, nor am I answerable for him. I would not dare to judge the spirit of the man, for that is a most difficult task, especially when it is a question of his condemnation. Yet, if I were favorably inclined to him as a good man, which even his enemies admit him to be, or as an accused person, which the laws permit even to sworn judges, or as one oppressed, following the dictates of humanity—indeed, as one oppressed by those who under the false pretext of being devout fight against learning—if I were inclined thus to take his part, what reproach would there be, provided I did not become involved myself in his cause? In short, I think it is only Christian to support Luther this far, for if he is innocent, I do not want him crushed by a faction of rogues, and if he is in error, I wish him to be corrected, not destroyed. This approach agrees better with the example of Christ, who, according to the prophet, did not extinguish the smoking flax, nor break the bruised reed.

I should wish that that heart, which seems to hold certain bright sparks of evangelical doctrine, be not crushed but rather be corrected and called to preach the glory of Christ. At the present moment, however, certain theologians with whom I am acquainted neither admonish nor instruct Luther; they only defame the man before the people with their insane cries and lacerate him with their savage and virulent abuse, speaking of nothing else but heresies and heretics. It cannot be denied that a most unpleasant outcry has been raised here among the people by persons who have not yet seen Luther's books. It is certain that some have expressly condemned what they have not understood. For example, Luther had written that we are not bound to confess mortal sins unless they are "manifest," meaning by that term "known to us when we confess." A certain Carmelite theologian,[4] explaining "manifest" in this context as sins "openly committed," shouted about this in an extraordinary fashion simply because he did not understand the question. It is certain that they have condemned as heretical in Luther's books statements which are regarded as orthodox and even edifying in the works of Bernard and Augustine.

I warned these men in the beginning to refrain from such outbursts and instead to present their case in writings and arguments. First, I advised them not to condemn publicly what they have not read, or rather what they have not seriously considered (I will not say what they have not understood). Secondly, I told them that it is unbecoming for theologians, whose judgment should carry great weight, to do anything by raising a commotion, and that they should

---

[4] This would appear to be Egmondanus, prior of the Carmelites at Louvain and one of Erasmus' most persistent critics.

not rage against a man whose life was approved by all.
Finally, I said that perhaps it is not safe to touch on such
topics before a mixed crowd, in which there are many to
whom the confession of secret sins is intensely displeasing.
If such persons hear that there are theologians who deny
that we have to confess all sins, they will quickly seize upon
and hold this perverse notion.

Although any judicious man would consider, as I did,
that this was sensible advice, nevertheless, as a result of
these friendly admonitions they conceived the idea that
Luther's books were for the most part mine and that they
were written at Louvain; yet there is not a letter in them that
is mine, nor were they published with my knowledge or
consent. Relying on this completely false suspicion, however,
and without bringing their complaints to me, they provoked
many tragic scenes here, worse than any I have seen thus
far in my life. Besides, while the proper task of theologians
is to instruct, I now observe that many do nothing but con-
strain or destroy and extinguish, though Augustine, even
in the case of the Donatists, who were not only heretics but
also savage brigands, does not approve of those who only
use force and do not instruct. Men, whom gentleness especially becomes, seem to thirst for nothing except human
blood, and they eagerly desire only that Luther be seized and
destroyed. But this is to play the part of the executioner, not
the theologian. If they wish to show themselves as great
theologians, let them convert the Jews, let them convert to
Christ those who are strangers to Christ, let them correct
the public morals of Christians, than which there is nothing
more corrupt, not even among the Turks. How is it right
that he should be carried off to punishment who in the first
place proposed for debate those propositions which the
theological schools have always debated and have even questioned? Why should he be struck down, who desires to be
taught, who submits to the judgment of the Apostolic See,

who entrusts himself to the judgment of the universities? And if he does not deliver himself into the hands of those who would rather destroy him than correct him, there should be no cause for surprise.

At the outset the sources of this evil must be examined. The world is weighed down with human ordinances, burdened with scholastic opinions and dogmas, oppressed by the tyranny of the mendicant friars, who, though they are attendants upon the Roman see, nevertheless have achieved such power and numbers that they are formidable to the Roman pontiff himself and even to kings. When the pope acts in their behalf, he is more than God; but when things work against their advantage, he is no more than a dream. I do not condemn all of them, but very many are of the kind who do their best to ensnare the consciences of men for their own profit and power. And, having set aside modesty, they had undertaken to preach, to the exclusion of Christ, nothing save their own new and increasingly more shameless dogmas. They preached indulgences in such a way that even the ignorant could not bear it. Due to this and many other similar causes, the vigor of the Gospel teaching was gradually disappearing. And it looked as if, with things ever heading for the worse, the spark of Christian piety, whence an extinct charity could be rekindled, would at last be totally put out. The sum of religion was tending towards a more than Jewish ceremonial. Good men bemoan and deplore all this. Even the theologians themselves, who are not monks, and even some monks, admit this in their private conversations.

It was this, in my opinion, which at first drove Luther to dare oppose the intolerable shamelessness of certain monks. How may I form any other opinion about him who seeks neither honors nor wealth? I am not questioning at present the propositions they object to in Luther, I am only discussing the kind they are and the occasion for them. Luther dared to challenge indulgences, but others previously had made rather extravagant assertions about them. He presumed to speak rather reservedly about the power of the Roman pontiff, but others had first written with far too little reserve about it, particularly three Dominicans: Alvarus, Sylvester, and the cardinal of San Sisto.[5] He dared to make little of the principles of Thomas, but the Dominicans almost prefer these to the Gospels. He ventured to disperse several scruples about the nature of confession, but here the monks endlessly ensnare men's consciences. He was bold enough to disregard to some extent scholastic principles, but the schoolmen themselves attribute too much to them, though they differ considerably among themselves about them and at the end repeatedly change their views, introducing new ideas in place of the old.

Pious minds were troubled when they heard in the universities scarcely any discussion of evangelical doctrine and observed that the sacred writers approved of old by the Church were now regarded as obsolete; and even in sermons they heard very little about Christ but much about the power of the pope and the opinions of modern authors. All this eloquence now openly displayed self-advantage, servility, ambition, and deceit. This must be blamed, in my opinion, even if Luther has written somewhat intemperately. Whoever favors evangelical doctrine, favors also the Roman pontiff, who is the chief herald of the Gospel, as the other bishops are the heralds of the same. All bishops serve in the place of Christ, but the Roman pontiff is pre-eminent among them. He must be considered as favoring nothing more than the glory of Christ, whose minister it is his glory to be. They deserve very ill of him who in their flattery attribute powers to him which he himself does not acknowledge and

---

[5] Alvarus Pelagius was a fourteenth-century Spanish theologian (and a Franciscan!). Sylvester Prierias was at this time the Master of the Papal Palace. He wrote a critical report for the Curia on the Ninety-five Theses in early 1518. The cardinal of San Sisto is the distinguished Cardinal Cajetan, who was at this time general of the Dominicans. As papal legate in Germany, he had interviewed Luther at the Diet of Augsburg in October 1518 and had subsequently pressed for Luther's apprehension.

which are not to the advantage of the Christian flock. And further, some who are behind these tragic scenes are not motivated by zeal for the pope, but they misuse his power for their own profit and supremacy. We have, so I think, a good pope. But in such a rush of events there is much of which he is ignorant; and there are certain things he cannot achieve, even if he wishes, for, as Virgil says, "the charioteer is borne by the horses, nor does the chariot respond to the reins." Therefore, he contributes to the virtue of his pontificate who encourages that which especially is worthy of Christ. It is plain, however, that there are those who incite His Holiness against Luther, and indeed against all who dare murmur against their dogmas. But the greatest princes should seek rather to know the lasting will of the pope than to show a deference extorted by base motives.

Moreover, I could most truthfully point out what kind of people the authors of this trouble are, but I fear that I should seem abusive, even though I continue to speak the truth. I know many of them intimately; many have revealed themselves in their published books, where their minds and their lives are reflected as clearly as in a mirror. Would that they who arrogate to themselves the censor's rod, whereby they expel from the Christian fold whom they will, would that they had deeply imbibed the teaching and spirit of Christ! This power belongs only to those who have purged themselves of all the filth of this world's lusts. Whether the men I speak of be such he will soon discover who treats with them on any matter which pertains to their profit, glory, or revenge. I wish that I could convince Your Highness of what I have observed and learned about these affairs, but it is fitting that I remember Christian restraint.

I speak of these things more freely because I am not involved in any way in the cause of Reuchlin and Luther. I myself neither wish to write thus, nor do I espouse that teaching so that I wish to defend what has been written by another; but I do not refrain from making this clear, that these trouble makers aim at something quite different than they publicly proclaim. For a long time they have been distressed that learning flourishes, that languages flourish, that the ancient authors, formerly covered with dust and consumed by the moth, are reviving, and that the world is being recalled to the sources themselves. They fear for their own shortcomings, they do not want to seem not to know something, they dread lest anything decrease their majesty. Though they concealed this ulcer a long while, it has, however, recently erupted, the pain of it all surpassing any concealment. Even before Luther's books appeared, they were already at work with great zeal, especially the Dominicans and the Carmelites. Would that many of them were not more villainous than untaught! When Luther's books were published, they grasped them as if they were a handle and used them to link the cause of language and learning, that of Reuchlin and of Luther, and indeed my own, together in the same bundle, presenting their case poorly as well as distinguishing badly between the objects of their attack. For what has literary study to do with a matter of faith? And how am I involved in the cause of Reuchlin and Luther? But by this trick they have mixed these things together so that they may burden all friends of learning with a common reproach.

Further, that this whole matter is not sincerely prosecuted may be surmised from what follows: Although they admit that there are no ancient or modern authors in which errors are not found, even errors that would make them heretical, if anyone should obstinately uphold them, why, with certain exceptions, do they investigate only this one or the other, and with such hatred? They do not deny that Alvarus, the cardinal of San Sisto, and Sylvester Prierias err in many places. No mention is made about them, for these men are Dominicans. The clamor is reserved for Reuchlin, because he has an excellent knowledge of languages, and for Luther, whom they believe endowed with our literary interests, although his attainments in this field are slight. Luther has written much that is more imprudent than impious; and they have taken it very ill that he has little regard for Thomas, that he reduces the profit from indulgences, that he takes small account of the mendicant orders, that he defers more to the Gospels than to scholastic dogma, and that he slights the refined quibbling of the debaters. These undoubtedly are the intolerable heresies. But they have disguised these complaints, and, crafty men united in the desire only to do harm, they conceal their hateful aims from the pope.

At one time the heretic was heard respectfully, and he was absolved if he made amends; but if he persisted in his heresy after his conviction, the extreme penalty was his exclusion from communion with the Church. Now the crime of heresy is a different matter, and yet for any trifling reason the cry is immediately raised, "This is heresy, this is heresy." Formerly he was a heretic who dissented from the Gospels, the articles of faith, or something of comparable authority. Now, if anyone disagrees in any way with Thomas, or even if anyone disagrees with a false theory which some sophist in the schools recently invented, he is called a heretic. Whatever is not pleasing, whatever they do not understand is a heresy. To know Greek is a heresy. To speak in a polished manner is a heresy. Whatever they themselves do not do is a heresy. I admit that the charge of a corrupted faith is grave, but it is not necessary to turn everything into a question of faith. And whoever treats matters of faith should be far removed from every taint of ambition, self-advantage, hatred, or revenge.

Who does not see what these men stand for and in what direction they are heading? Once the restraints on their evil passions are relaxed, they will begin to rage indiscriminately against every good man, and finally they will threaten the bishops themselves and even the Roman pontiff. I will not deny that this charge would seem to be a false one, except that we see certain individuals already doing this.

What the Dominicans have dared to do, Savonarola and the villainous affair at Berne, not to mention anything else, should serve as a warning to us.[6] I am not going to reopen the disgraceful story of that order, but I warn what we must be on guard against if these men should succeed in what they rashly attempt.

What I have said thus far is aside from the cause itself of Luther. I am discussing only the manner of dealing with it and the danger therein to us all. The Roman pontiff has reserved Reuchlin's case for his own judgment. The affair of Luther has been transferred to the universities. Whatever verdict they will render will not threaten me. I have always taken care not to write anything offensive or seditious or alien to the teachings of Christ. I shall never knowingly teach error or cause confusion; I would endure anything sooner than provoke dissension. Nevertheless, I wished that Your Eminence be informed about certain matters, not that I presume to give advice or command, but that if the adversaries of learning should attempt to hide behind your dignity, the best course of action on these matters can more surely be determined; but, in my opinion, the more one keeps out of this business, the more directly he preserves his own peace. I have revised the *Methodus* which I dedicated to Your Highness, and I greatly enlarged it. May the All good and All powerful Christ ever keep Your Excellency safe and flourishing.

ERASMUS OF ROTTERDAM

Louvain, October 19, 1519

[6] The reference to Savonarola is interesting in this context. Erasmus considers the fiery Dominican preacher of Florence as disobeying and defying the pope. The "villainous affair at Berne" refers to some bogus apparitions which the Dominicans had engineered there in 1507-9 and the attempted poisoning of their dupe. They were exposed and punished. See Allen, IV, 106.

VII

The *Axiomata*

This interesting document consists of twenty-two axioms or statements concerning the controversy over Martin Luther.[1] It was drawn
up by Erasmus for the guidance of Luther's prince, Elector Frederick
of Saxony, following an interview with the Elector at Cologne on
November 5, 1520.[2] Both Erasmus and Frederick were in Cologne in
the entourage of Emperor Charles V, who had been crowned at
Aachen in late October and was now en route to Worms for a meeting
of the imperial Diet. Frederick at this moment was again being
pressed by the papal representatives to imprison Luther or to turn
him over to the higher ecclesiastical authorities. In this situation he
sought the advice of the distinguished scholar. Immediately after the
interview that advice was drafted in the terse form of the *Axiomata*
and given to Spalatin, the Elector's secretary and Luther's friend, for
transmission to the Elector. There can be little doubt that Erasmus'
counsel, so favorable to Luther, confirmed and encouraged Frederick
in his policy of protecting Luther at this critical juncture.

The *Axiomata* are also one of the last expressions of a truly pro-
Lutheran stance on the part of Erasmus. After 1520 Erasmus' hope
of a peaceful settlement of the controversy and his efforts in that
direction seemed a lost cause, or at least a disheartening and forlorn
endeavor. Luther had by then assumed a defiant and extreme position
beyond the hope of compromise (as witness his *The Babylonian*

---

[1] The Latin text is in *Erasmi opuscula,* ed. W. K. Ferguson (The Hague,
1933), pp. 336–37. The present translation was made by the editor.

[2] See Ferguson's introduction to the *Axiomata,* ibid., pp. 329–33 and Allen,
IV, 370–71. For an appraisal of the *Axiomata* in the general context of the
Erasmus–Luther relationship, see C. R. Thompson's introduction to his edition
of Erasmus' *Inquisitio de Fide,* pp. 19–23.

Captivity of the Church of October 1520 and his burning of the bull *Exsurge Domine* on December 10, 1520), and in 1521 his formal excommunication by the Church and his banning by the Empire were pronounced.

The *Axiomata* were not intended for publication, and Erasmus was quite concerned lest they fall into the hands of Cardinal Aleander, the papal legate, who also was in Cologne at this time. But, like the letter to Albert of Brandenburg on Luther, they were soon in print—in a pamphlet issuing from Leipzig within a month or so after they were written.

Axioms of Erasmus of Rotterdam in behalf of the cause of Martin Luther, theologian

The origin of the case is evil: the hatred of letters and the desire for supremacy.

The way in which it is being conducted corresponds to the origin, with wild cries, plots, bitter hatred, poisonous writing.

Those who are conducting the case are open to suspicion.

Since all the best and closest to the Gospel teaching are said to be the least offended by Luther.

It is well known that certain men take advantage of the good nature of the Pope.

All the more should their rash advice on this case be shunned.

The case is tending toward a greater crisis than certain men suppose.

The severity of the bull offends all upright men as unworthy of the most gentle vicar of Christ.[3]

---

[3] The bull referred to is the *Exsurge Domine,* promulgated by Pope Leo X on June 15, 1520. Forty-one of Luther's statements were condemned and he was given sixty days after the bull was posted in Germany to recant or be excommunicated.

All the more diligently should it be considered by persons who are above suspicion and who are experienced in these matters.

Only two universities out of such a countless number have condemned Luther, and they have merely condemned him, not convicted him of error; nor are they in agreement.[4]

He himself seems to all fair men to seek what is fair, since he offers himself for public debate and submits to judges who are above suspicion.

Those who attack Luther introduce that which offends pious ears.

But he who makes himself a judge or censurer should himself be without blame.

Luther is not soliciting anything; therefore he is less suspect.

The interest of others is being pressed.

For the pope the glory of Christ comes before his own, and what is of profit to souls takes precedence over any other advantage.

Although these matters ought especially to be discussed, it was fitting however that this be done at another time.

Difficult matters press upon us, and the guidance of Charles should not be defiled by such hateful measures.[5]

It seems to the advantage of the pope that this affair be settled by the mature deliberation of serious and impartial

---

[4] The theological faculty at Cologne condemned eight of Luther's statements on August 30, 1519. The theologians at Louvain followed suit in their condemnation of November 7, 1519, though, as Erasmus points out, the opinions condemned at Louvain differed from those condemned at Cologne.

[5] Charles, of course, is Emperor Charles V, who was soon to preside at the Diet of Worms where the question of Luther was to be discussed. Erasmus is obviously asking for calm and impartial judgment.

men; in this way will regard best be shown for the dignity of the pope.

Those who up to now have written against Luther are disapproved even by theologians who otherwise are opposed to Luther.

The world thirsts for the Gospel truth, and it seems to be carried in this direction by a longing ordained, as it were, by fate.

Therefore, since it so happens, opposition [to Luther] ought to be without hate.

VIII

Letter to Jodocus Jonas on Luther

MAY 10, 1521

Erasmus wrote this letter to Jodocus Jonas a few weeks after Luther appeared before the imperial Diet of Worms to answer charges of heresy in his writings.[1] Jonas (1493–1555), a professor at the University of Erfurt, had accompanied Luther to Worms and was now more or less his committed disciple. Erasmus, who had met Jonas two years before, was writing to dissuade him from going over wholeheartedly to the Lutheran camp. The tone of this letter is in sharp contrast to that of the earlier letter to Albert of Brandenburg and of the *Axiomata,* and unlike these previous statements, it castigates the immoderation of Luther and warns of the danger he poses to the peace of the Church and the progress of true reform.

In this letter to Jonas and in the one which follows it in this volume, Erasmus "did what he could to hold him back . . . but without avail."[2] Jonas left Erfurt in June 1521 to take up residence at Wittenberg and to become a professor of theology at the university there. He married the following year, wrote a *Defensio pro conjugio sacerdotali,* and, along with Philip Melanchthon, became one of Luther's closest associates. Erasmus wrote in early 1524 that he had defected from "our brotherhood" and that he had warned Jonas and other defectors in vain.[3]

This letter is a companion to the one which appears here as Selection IX, wherein Erasmus continues his argument, though in a different way, against Jonas' adherence to the Lutheran cause. Both letters were published by Froben in 1521 in Erasmus' *Epistolae ad diversos.*

---

[1] The Latin text is in Allen, IV, 486–93. The present translation was made by the editor from Allen.

[2] Allen, III, 413.

[3] Letter to Conrad Mutianus (Allen, V, 110).

To Jodocus Jonas,
GREETINGS FROM ERASMUS OF ROTTERDAM:

There is a rumor persistent here for a long time now, dear Jonas, that at Worms you were with Martin Luther continuously; nor do I doubt that your sense of duty prompted this, as I should have urged if it happened that I were present, so that this tragedy might be so settled on reasonable grounds that in the future it could not erupt again with greater evil for the world. For my part I wonder that that was not accomplished, since this achievement would have been very agreeable to the best men, who, as is worthy of souls truly Christian, desired that the tranquillity of the Church be taken into account, the name "church" being lost if concord is not joined to it. For what else is our religion than peace in the Holy Spirit? Furthermore, the orthodox Fathers testify that in former times the church of Christ was afflicted with great vices, because thus far it embraces good fish and bad in the same net and is forced to endure the cockle mixed with the wheat; and they repeatedly lamented the most corrupt morals of those orders from whom it was proper that examples of an inherent piety proceed. Moreover, when the Roman church in times gone by departed from a devotion to evangelical purity, this was made clear enough either by Jerome, who calls it the Babylon of the Apocalypse, or by Saint Bernard in the books which he entitled *De consideratione*—although there have not been wanting also among modern authors, men of celebrated name, who have demanded the public renewal of ecclesiastical discipline.

Yet I do not know whether the princes of the Church have ever coveted the privileges of this world, which Christ taught should be despised, with so much zeal and so openly as we see today. Nor had the study of Sacred Scripture sunk lower than morals themselves. Divine literature was forced to be the servant of human ambition, the credulity of the people was turned to the profit of the few. Pious minds, to whom nothing is more important than the glory of Christ, groaned at the sight of this. And the result was that in the beginning Luther had as much approbation on all sides as, I believe, has come to any mortal for several centuries past. For, as we easily believe what we ardently desire, they thought that a man had arisen who, free from all the attachments of this world, could bring some remedy for such great evils. Nor was I entirely without hope, except that immediately at the first sampling of the tracts which had begun to appear under Luther's name I was quite afraid that the matter might end in tumult and general dissidence throughout the world. And so through my letters I at one time warned Luther himself, then friends of his whose authority I thought would have force with him. I do not know what advice they gave him; in any event the matter was handled in such a way that there is the danger that because of the attempt to apply remedies improperly, the evil for us may be doubled.

And I greatly wonder, my dear Jonas, what god has stirred up the heart of Luther, in so far as he assails with such license of pen the Roman pontiff, all the universities, philosophy, and the mendicant orders. Even if all were true, which those who undertake to judge Luther's writings say is by no means the case, what other outcome could be expected, because of the provocation of so many, than this which we see? Up to now I have not had the time to read Luther's books, but on the basis of those which I have sampled and what in passing I have sometimes gathered from the report of others, although it was not within my competence, perhaps, to pronounce on the truth of the opinions which were advanced, certainly the manner and method of going about the business were by no means approved by me. For when in itself an issue is a matter of bitter truth to very many, and when in itself a turbulent issue usually leads, by long experience, to violent upheaval, it were better to mitigate through courteous treatment an issue sharp by its very nature than to add ill will to ill will.

What purpose did it serve, therefore, to act in a contrary way and to expose certain matters in such a way that at first sight they were even more offensive than when seen at closer and steadier range? For some things even in deliberate obscurity, as it were, are troublesome. What was achieved by raging with such fierce outcries? If it was against those he desired to correct, his method must be attributed to imprudence; but if it was against those he wished to provoke to evil everywhere, his method should be attributed to impiety. Moreover, although it is the part of the experienced steward to dispense the truth, that is, to bring it forth when the occasion demands, and to bring forth enough of it, and to bring forth what is suitable for each, he poured out everything at the same time in so many pamphlets cast forth headlong, divulging everything and making public even to cobblers what is usually treated among the learned as mysterious and secret; and frequently by some unbridled impulse, in my opinion, at least, he is carried beyond what is just. For example, he calls the whole philosophy of Aristotle the death of the soul, when it was sufficient to remind theologians that they too are entangled in Peripatetic, or rather sophist, philosophy.

That evangelical spirit of Christ has its own prudence, it has its own courtesy and gentleness. Thus even Christ accommodated himself to the temperaments of the Jews. He speaks one thing to the more uncultivated crowds, another to the disciples, and he gradually leads these very men, bearing with them for a long time, to an understanding of heavenly philosophy. With this in mind he bids his disciples that they first preach penance and the imminent kingdom of God, that they not speak of Christ. Thus Peter, in the

Acts of the Apostles, with words that are gentle and loving, not abusive, adds so great a multitude as the first fruits to the Church.[4] He does not scream at those who had killed Christ, he does not magnify in dreadful language their wicked madness, although it is probable that there were in that number men who had brought Christ to death. But, as if assuaging them, he says that this was thus accomplished by the divine purpose; then he even casts the impiety of the crime back on the age itself. "Save yourselves," he says, "from this perverse generation." He does not hurl back abuse at those who said the Apostles were drunk with new wine, but he offers reasonable explanations: it is the energy of a new spirit, not of wine. He quotes the testimony of Joel, which he knew would have very much weight among them. And not yet does he proclaim Christ God and Man; he reserved this mystery for its own time. Meanwhile he calls Him the just man, he proclaims Him Lord and Messiah, and he does this on the authority of the God whom these men also piously worshiped, so that from the Father whom they acknowledged he might win favor for the Son. Moreover, when he made known that the statement which they understood about David was said of Christ, not of David, softening the words that would be offensive, he says, "Brothers, let me say to you freely of the patriarch David."

Thus Paul becomes all things to all men, so he might win all to Christ, instructing his disciples to teach with all gentleness, not estranging anyone by harshness of manner and speech, but overcoming with gentleness even the ill-tempered and the rude. With what great courtesy he preaches Christ to the Athenians, casting back their faults on the age itself.[5] "The times of this ignorance God has, it is true, overlooked," he says. In an appropriate and pleasing introduc-

---

[4] The reference is to St. Peter's discourse in Acts 2.
[5] Acts 17:22 ff.

tion he calls them "men of Athens." Nor does he with fierce
words rail at their wicked cult of demons, but with courteous
speech he accuses them of excessive observance who have
worshiped more than they ought. He turns the inscription on
the altar, which he observed by chance, into an argument for
the faith, after he had indeed changed and pruned some of
the words; nor does he thus far call Christ other than the
Man through whom God has chosen to bestow salvation
on all mankind; nor does he quote among them the testimony
of the Prophets, which would have very little weight, but he
speaks to them of the testimony of Aratus. With what great
urbanity does he plead his case before Festus and Agrippa![6]

Thus Augustine refutes the frenzied Donatists and the
more than mad Manichaeans, so that he both becomes angry
within the merits of the case and mingles the sweetness of
his charity everywhere, thirsting for their salvation, not their
destruction. Gentleness in teaching these doctrines, the
prudence of divine discourse in dispensing them captured the
world and, what no arms, no philosophical subtlety, no ora-
torical eloquence, no human power or skill could ever do,
brought it under the yoke of Christ. All the more does it
behoove us, if we desire to do good, to refrain from all
violent reproaches, especially if we take issue with those who
are prominent because of their public authority. Paul
wished that honor be given magistrates, even those that were
heathen; and he recanted, as it were, because he had spoken
ill of the openly wicked Mosaic high priest.[7] He wished
slaves who had become Christian to submit to their heathen
masters even more scrupulously than they had done before;
he wished wives by their profession of Christ to be even
more obedient to their irreverent husbands, for no other
reason than that by the forbearance of their conduct they

6 Acts 26.
7 Acts 23:2-5.

might entice all to the love of the Gospel teaching. He who has a pious mind desires only to do good, either proceeding in silence if there is no hope, or disclosing and dispensing the truth in such a way that he does not intensify the disease rather than cure it.

Brutus was indignant at Cicero for provoking those in his speeches and writings whom he could not hold in check when provoked. Deceit and dissimulation in the philosopher-prince was not displeasing to Plato, provided that his wiles were employed for the public good. It is proper, I confess, that the Christian be free from every deceit; but nevertheless it happens sometimes that the truth may well be silent, and everywhere it is a matter of great importance when, among whom, and by what means the truth is disclosed. Trustworthy physicians do not immediately have recourse to extreme remedies. They first prescribe gentler drugs for the ill body; and they regulate the dosage in such a way that they may restore it to health, not bury it. Nor do I agree with those who say that the illness of this present time is too serious to be healed with gentle remedies. According to the Greek proverb, it is better for an evil to lie as it is, rather than to be disturbed by improper remedies.

Indeed, I do not deny that God sometimes corrects his flock by war, pestilence, and suffering; it is not for the pious, however, to cause war and wicked torment, if God at times turns the misfortune of others into a good for his own. The cross of Christ brought salvation to the world, and yet we execrate those who brought Him to the cross. The death of the martyrs adorned and at the same time strengthened the church of God; nevertheless, the wickedness of those through whom this good has come to us has been condemned. Many would be less wicked if they were deprived of their riches. It is not for the upright man, however, to despoil anyone of his possessions in order to make him better. Moreover, since everything new and unusual gives rise to a

disturbance, even when there is a call to better things, if anything differs from what is customary, it must be proposed in
such a way that it appears to differ as little as possible.

Yet it is said that Luther, although he teaches the same
doctrine as others, several times endeavors by the very
language he uses, so it would seem, to make it appear that he
asserts the most dissimilar views. Moreover, as men's be-
havior is inclined to the worse, their vices must be so corrected that the occasion for sinning more freely is not offered
to others. Paul preaches evangelical liberty as against the
ruinous servitude of the law, but he adds, "Only do not use
liberty as an occasion for sensuality."[8] He exhorts against
the cold works of the law so that he may incessantly encourage to works of charity. Perhaps there were some who
out of honest zeal favored calling the orders and princes of
the Church to better things. But I do not know if they are
those who under this pretext covet the wealth of the church-
men. I judge nothing to be more wicked and destructive of
public tranquillity than this. For if they believe it is right to
seize the property of priests because some consume their
wealth in extravagant living or otherwise spend it for purposes not too honorable, not many citizens or magnates will
find the possession of their goods sufficiently secure. This
certainly is a fine turn of affairs, if property is wickedly taken
away from priests so that soldiers may make use of it in
worse fashion; and the latter squander their own wealth, and
sometimes that of others, so that no one benefits.

I do not even agree with those men, my dear Jonas, who
say that Luther, provoked by the intolerable shamelessness
of his adversaries, could not maintain a Christian moderation. Regardless of how others conduct themselves, he who
had undertaken such a role ought to be faithful to himself
and disregard all other matters. Finally, a way out should
have been provided before he descended into that pit, lest

8 Galatians 5:13.

there occur what happened to the goat in the fable. Even in
pious matters it is foolish to begin what you cannot finish,
especially if a not too fortunate attempt brings the greatest
misfortune instead of the advantages that were desired. We
see the affair brought to that point that I reasonably see no
good outcome, unless Christ through His own skill turn the
rashness of these men into a public good.

Some excuse Luther because, forced by the incitement of
others, he first wrote more violently and then did not entrust
himself to the judgment of most clement Leo and of Emperor Charles, by far the noblest and most gentle prince of
the faith. But why was he more disposed to give ear to these
inciters than to other friends, neither unlearned nor inexperienced in affairs, urging him along different paths? With
what kind of defense, I ask, did a great many who favored
him attempt to protect him? With ridiculous little books and
with empty threats. As if, in fact, this type of nonsense either
frightens his adversaries or attracts good men, to whose
judgment the whole affair should have been made to conform, provided that they wished their stories to mark a fruit-
ful turning point. How great a swarm of evils this foolhardi-
ness now yields! And ill will greatly weighs down the study
of letters as well as many good men who in the beginning
were not particularly hostile to Luther, either because they
hoped he would handle the matter differently or on account
of the enemies they had in common. For it happened by
some chance that those who at the outset made trouble for
Luther were enemies of learning, and on this account the
devotees of letters were less hostile to Luther lest by
supporting the ranks of his adversaries they strengthen the
power of their own enemies. Although, whatever the case
may be, the care of religion must take precedence over that
of studies.

And here, my dear Jonas, I have been forced at times to
wish for evidence of the evangelical spirit when I saw

Luther, but especially his supporters, strive with skill, as it
were, to involve others in a hateful and dangerous affair.
For what did it avail to have Reuchlin, burdened enough
thus far, weighed down with heavier ill will? What was the
need to make mention, so often invidious, of my name, when
the case by no means demanded it? I have advised Luther
in a private and sealed letter; it was soon printed at Leipzig.[9]
I had advised the Cardinal of Mainz in a sealed letter lest
he rashly surrender Luther, whose cause thus far was praiseworthy to most good men, to the wanton pleasure of certain
ones.[10] It was published before it was delivered. Pirckheimer
complains in his letter to me that certain letters are circulat-
ing in printed form which no one ever delivered to him.[11] In
these they urge him to continue steadfastly in what he had
begun, so that it is clear that they drag him, whether he
wishes or not, into the fellowship of that faction.

They extracted certain offensive passages which seemed
to have a relationship to some of Luther's tenets from books
I wrote before I dreamed that Luther would arise, and they
published them in German.[12] And those who do this wish to
be considered friends, although a mortal enemy could do
nothing more hostile. The men who wish me the most ill
have not had as much ingenuity in injuring me. They have
presented this weapon to my enemies so that now in public
sermons they might proclaim where I agree with Luther.
As if, indeed, falsehood may not be the neighbor on both
sides of truth, if you go beyond the mark! I somewhere
warn, perhaps, that vows should not rashly be made, and I

[9] Erasmus' letter to Luther of May 30, 1519, is in Huizinga, op. cit., pp.
229-31.

[10] Selection VI.

[11] Willibald Pirckheimer (1470-1530) was a German scholar and humanist
whose attitude toward Luther at this time was similar to that of Erasmus. See
Allen, IV, 491.203n, regarding this reference.

[12] Erasmus may refer here to his letter to Volz (Selection V), which
Spalatin translated into German in 1520 and which was published about this
time.

disapprove of those who run off to the shrine of St. James or to Jerusalem, where they had no business, and leave at home their wife and children, whose life and virtue should have been their chief concern. I warn that young men should not be enticed into the bonds of the religious life before they know themselves and know what the religious life is. Luther, so they say, totally condemns all vows. I complain somewhere that the burden of confession has been made heavier by the subtleties of certain men. Luther, so they say, teaches that all confession should be rejected as a dangerous institution. I have taught somewhere that the best authors should be read first, adding that as much profit may not be gained from the books of Dionysius as their titles appear to promise.[13] Luther calls the man absurd, I hear, and unworthy of being read at all.

This is indeed a fine state of agreement, if, going beyond the limit of my words, another distorts what I have properly written at a favorable time and with moderation. The laws, however, would be most unjust to me if I should be held responsible lest anyone in the future also abuse my writings. This fate did not even befall the Apostle Paul, if we are to believe his colleague Peter![14] Nevertheless, to speak frankly, if I had foreseen that an age such as this would arise, either I would not have written certain things which I did write, or I would have written them in a different way. For I desire to be of service to all in such a way that no one is injured, if that is possible. Little books composed by conspirators, in which Erasmus also is portrayed, are circulated. However, no name is more hateful to me than that of conspiracy or schism or faction.

This whole affair, whatever the story is, has been started against my advice, or at least with my constant disapproval

---

[13] Dionysius the Areopagite was the supposed author of several theological works highly regarded in the Middle Ages, including *On the Heavenly and Ecclesiastical Hierarchies, On the Divine Names,* and *On Mystical Theology.*

[14] 2 Peter 3:16.

of the manner employed. My letters have never served any
faction other than that of Christ, whom we all have in
common. I do not know what influence I have by this mode
of thinking and by these letters; certainly I have tried and
I desire to be of service not only to the Germans but to the
French, the Spanish, the English, the Bohemians, the Rus-
sians, and indeed to the Turks and Saracens as well, if possible. So far am I from ever having wished to be involved
in a faction as dangerous as this! And in the meantime I
also look for prudence among those who believe that by
tricks of this kind anyone can be enticed into their camp. If
they wish to alienate any judicious man, by what method
might they better do this? But they proclaim enough that this
is a weak support, as they say, although they put their trust
in such aid in so hazardous an affair. Moreover, I am desperately afraid lest among the other nations this affair
bring a great disgrace to our Germany, as the great mass of
men are accustomed to impute the foolishness of a few to the
entire nation.

What else has been accomplished, therefore I ask, by so
many harsh little books, by so much foolish talk, by so many
formidable threats, and by so much bombast save that what
was previously debated in the universities as probable opinion may be hereafter an article of faith, and that then
indeed it may be scarcely safe to teach the Gospel, while
everything is seized and misrepresented because all have
been exasperated? Luther could have taught the evangelical
philosophy with great profit to the Christian flock, he could
have benefited the world by bringing forth books, if he had
restrained from those things which could only end in disturbance. He has also taken away from my works a good
part of the profit they contained. Not even the disputations
in the universities, which used to be most frank, are free. If
it is right to hate anyone because of personal offences, the
Lutherans have injured no one more than me. And yet I

would desire, in spite of that, that this discord, by far the most dangerous, be adjusted, and be adjusted in such a way that it does not break out later with more serious peril, as an ulcer often does that has been badly treated.

Will you tell me, dear Jonas, why you have given me the occasion for this now tardy complaint? First, because, although the affair has gone on longer than it should have, yet even now one may watch for the opportunity of quieting so great a disturbance. We have a pontiff who is by his very nature most clement, we have an emperor endowed with a mild and placable disposition. If it cannot be done, I do not wish you to entangle yourself in this trouble. I have always loved in you the splendid gifts of Christ: all the more I wish that you be saved for the work of the Gospel. And the more I loved the inborn ability of Hutten, the more I grieve that it was snatched away from us by these disorders.[15] Who, indeed, would not be distressed in spirit if Philip Melanchthon, a youth provided with so many exceptional gifts, was deprived of the public good will of the learned by this storm?[16] For if certain things offend them with regard to those by whose will human affairs are governed, I am of the opinion that the latter must be left to their Lord. If they prescribe what is right, it is proper to obey; but if what is unjust, it is a holy act to bear it lest anything worse happen. If this age does not bring forth the whole Christ, it is, however, something to preach Him to the extent that one may.

These matters which I now discuss with you, dear Jonas, I would like you to discuss with Philip, or with any others like Philip. Above all, I am of the opinion that discord, ruinous for all, must be avoided. And that thus by what I

[15] Ulrich von Hutten (1488-1523), German knight and scholar, was an enthusiastic supporter of Luther. He and Erasmus had been friends, but the Lutheran issue was now provoking a bitter quarrel between them.
[16] Philip Melanchthon (1497-1560) became professor of Greek at Wittenberg in 1518. Though he was one of Luther's closest associates, he and Erasmus remained on good terms.

might call a holy artfulness the needs of the time must be served, that by no means the treasury of the Gospel truth be betrayed, whence can come the reformation of corrupt public morals. Perhaps someone will ask whether I have another mind regarding Luther than I had formerly. No, indeed, I have the same mind. I have always wished that, with changes made of certain things which were displeasing to me, he discuss purely the Gospel philosophy, from which the morals of our age have departed, alas, too far. I have always preferred that he be corrected rather than suppressed. I desired him to carry on the work of Christ in such a way that the leaders of the Church either approved or certainly not disapproved. I desired that Luther be loved openly and without danger. Nor do I have a different mind about my wrangling critics than about him. If they should preach Christ as piously as they rage against me impiously, I would forget what they accomplish in my case, and I will admire their zeal in Christ. I will not detest those babblers, if they begin to herald Christ. Farewell.

Louvain, May 10, 1521

IX

Letter to Jodocus Jonas
on Vitrier and Colet

JUNE 13, 1521

This second letter to Jonas is a logical companion to the first one.[1] Written a month later, it continues Erasmus' argument that Jonas should avoid the extravagances of Luther and should work for reform within the framework of the old Church. Whereas the first letter is a direct appeal, the second one approaches its theme in a somewhat oblique but nevertheless most meaningful way. Erasmus presents Jonas with the picture of two reformers—"two men of our age whom I consider to have been true and sincere Christians"—who from within the Church devoted their energies to evangelical renewal and reform. Erasmus' intent is quite obvious, and at the beginning of his letter as well as at its close Erasmus indicates that he is giving Jonas examples that he may well consider and imitate.

The two men who are sketched in this letter are Jehan Vitrier, a Franciscan friar whom Erasmus had met in 1501 at the Franciscan house at St. Omer in Artois, and John Colet, the famous English scholar and dean of St. Paul's in London. Vitrier is known chiefly from this letter to Jonas and from a reference in the Botzheim

---

[1] The Latin text is in Allen, IV, 507-27. The English translation presented here with some modification of spelling and punctuation is from Erasmus, *The Lives of Jehan Vitrier and John Colet,* trans. J. H. Lupton (London, 1883), pp. 1-47. The Lupton translation was made from *Erasmi opera omnia,* ed. Johannes Clericus (Leyden, 1703-1706), III, No. 435 and is the first of the entire Jonas letter to be published. It is accompanied in its original edition by extensive notes, but these have not been reprinted here. The notes appended here are by the editor.

Catalogue where Erasmus speaks of him as approving his early *Enchiridion*.[2] Colet (c. 1466–1519), of course, is very well known.[3] Distinguished as a scriptural scholar, he had been a close friend of Erasmus ever since Erasmus' first trip to England in 1499. In 1510 he had founded St. Paul's School, which Erasmus describes in this letter. Erasmus' sketch of Colet is a biographical document of considerable importance, and it ranks with the famous sketch of Thomas More which Erasmus sent to Ulrich von Hutten in 1519.[4]

TO JODOCUS JONAS OF ERFURT,
GREETINGS FROM ERASMUS OF ROTTERDAM:

With your earnest request, my worthy friend, that I would briefly portray for you, as in miniature, the life of John Colet, I will gladly comply; and the rather, from an impression that you are trying to find some eminent pattern of religion by which to regulate your own course of life. I have been acquainted with many persons, my dear Jonas, whose high principles I greatly esteemed; but I must own that I never yet saw any one in whose character I did not after all miss some trait of Christian sincerity when compared with the single-mindedness of the two whom I am about to describe.

It was my fortune to become acquainted with the former of them at a town in Artois commonly called St. Omer, at the time when the plague (in this respect, at least, of service to me) had driven me there from Paris. The latter I met within England, to which country I had been drawn by attachment to my patron Mountjoy.

If I give you two portraits instead of one, you will be the gainer; and to that, I know, you have no objection.

The first of the two was named Jehan Vitrier. He was of

2 Allen, I, 20.
3 On Colet, see Harbison, op. cit., pp. 55 ff; J. H. Lupton, *A Life of John Colet* (London, 1887) ; and Seebohm, op. cit.
4 The More sketch in English translation may be found in Huizinga, op. cit., pp. 231–39, and Nichols, III, 387–401.

the Franciscan order, having lighted on this way of life in his youth. And in no other respect, I should say, was he to be deemed inferior to Colet than that from the restrictions of his system his sphere of usefulness was more limited. He was about forty-four years of age when our acquaintance began; and unlike as our dispositions were, he became attached to me at once. With men of worth his influence was always very great, and many people of rank valued him most highly. In person he was tall and well-proportioned, of a happily constituted nature, high-spirited, yet most courteous withal. In his youth he had drunk deeply of the subtleties of Scotus. And without setting any great value on these, he yet did not wholly disparage them, as containing some things well put, though in uncouth phrase. But when he had the fortune to make acquaintance with Ambrose and Cyprian and Jerome, his relish for the other became very small in comparison. There was no writer on theology whose genius he more admired than Origen's. And on my objecting that I was surprised to see him take pleasure in the writings of a heretic, I was struck with the animation with which he replied that a mind from which there had issued so many works fraught with such learning and fervor could not but have been a dwelling place of the Holy Spirit.

He by no means approved of the system of life which he had entered by chance, or had been drawn into in the inexperience of youth. I have repeatedly heard him say that to sleep and wake and return to sleep again by the sound of a bell, to talk and leave off talking, to come and go, to eat and desist from eating, to do everything, in short, by man's injunction instead of by the rule of Christ, was the life of idiots rather than of religious men. Nothing, he would aver, was more unreasonable than equality among men so unequal, especially seeing that, buried beneath the rites and ordinances of man's invention, or even devoured with spleen, were often to be found minds of heavenly temper, minds born for better things. Yet at no time did he either counsel anyone else to change this way of life, or attempt anything of the kind himself, being ready to bear all things sooner than be a stumbling block in anyone's way. In this too he would copy the example of his beloved Paul. There was indeed nothing so unreasonable that he would not cheerfully put up with in his desire for the preservation of peace.

He had so thoroughly learnt by heart the books of Holy Scripture, St. Paul's Epistles more particularly, that he had the words of his favorite, St. Paul, completely at his finger ends. At whatever passage you set him on, he would, after a moment's thought, go on right through the Epistle without a single mistake. He remembered also considerable portions of St. Ambrose. And it is almost past belief how much he recollected of other orthodox writers of antiquity as well. This advantage he owed in part to a naturally good memory and in part to constant practice.

I once asked him in the course of conversation what his way of mental preparation was before going into the pulpit. He answered that it was his custom to take up St. Paul, and to spend the time reading him till he felt his heart grow warm. He would continue thus engaged, with the addition of fervent prayers to God, till warned that it was time for him to begin.

As a rule, he did not divide his sermons under heads. Most preachers, indeed, do this as if no other course were open to them, the result being in many cases a stiff and formal subdivision. And yet all this care about subdivision does but make the discourse cold and stiff and lessen our confidence in the preacher by the artifice it betrays. But Vitrier would so link together the Epistle and Gospel that had been read, in an unbroken flow of eloquence, as to send his hearers home both better instructed and more ardent in the pursuit of religion. With no unbecoming gesticulation, with nothing exciting or declamatory, but perfectly under control, his delivery was yet such that you felt the words to proceed from a fervent and sincere, yet a sober spirit withal. On no occasion did he preach to a wearisome length, nor did he make a parade of citing a variety of names, in the way that some do. For these will tack together formal extracts now from Scotus, Aquinas, and Durandus, now from canon and civil law doctors, or again from the philosophers or the poets, that the people may think they know everything. The discourse he delivered would be all full of Holy Scripture, and his tongue could run on nothing else. His heart was in his subject. He was possessed, good soul, with an enthusiastic desire of drawing men to the pure wisdom of Christ.

It was by labors such as these that he aspired to the glory of martyrdom. Nay more, he had once, as I learnt from his most intimate friends, obtained leave from his superiors to visit countries where Christ is either unknown or worshiped amiss, deeming his end a happy one if in the discharge of his duty he should have earned the martyr's crown. But when already on his way, he was recalled by hearing, as it were, a voice from heaven saying: "Return, John; thou wilt not want for martyrdom among thine own people." He obeyed the admonition, and soon found the truth of what that voice had foretold.

There was in his neighborhood a convent of nuns in which the whole system of religious life had sunk to such a low ebb that it was in truth a house of ill fame rather than a convent. Not but that there were some among them both capable and desirous of amendment. While seeking to recall these to Christ by frequent addresses and exhortations, a plot was laid against him by eight abandoned ones of the number. Having waylaid their victim, they dragged him to a secluded spot and there flung their wimples about him and tried to strangle him. Nor did they desist until some chance passersby interposed and stopped their criminal outrage.

The injured man was by that time unconscious, and breathing was with difficulty restored. Yet he made no complaint
about the matter in any quarter, not even to his most intimate acquaintances, nor omitted any service in which he was
accustomed to minister to the spiritual welfare of those
nuns. Nay, even the very looks with which he regarded them
never showed any unwonted sternness. He was well acquainted with the instigator of the plot, a Dominican, suffra-
gan bishop of Boulogne, a man of notoriously wicked life.
Yet he never troubled him either with any words about the
matter, though there was no class of men to whom he was
less favourably disposed than to such as, being religious-
teachers and guides by profession, by their wicked life and
doctrine estranged people from Christ.

I have known him preach as many as seven times in one
day, nor so long as Christ was to be his theme did a fund
of words full of matter ever fail him. In truth, his whole
life was nothing else than one continued sermon. At table
he was lively and without the least tinge of austerity, yet
still in such a way as never to show any signs of frivolity or
indecorum, much less of wantonness or excess. He would
season the repast with learned conversation, generally on
sacred subjects and conducive to religion. Such was his way
of talking, if he received or paid a visit. But if on a journey
—when some of the influential friends he had would often
lend him a horse or mule to ride on, for the sake of having
a more convenient chat with him on the road—on such an
occasion the good man would brighten up and let fall sayings more precious than any jewels. He let no one ever go
away from him disconsolate, no one that was not rather the
better for his visit and more encouraged to love religion.
There was nothing to make you feel that he studied any
private interests of his own. Neither gluttony, nor ambition,
nor covetousness, nor love of pleasure, nor enmity, nor
jealousy, nor any other bad passions held him under their

sway. He thanked God all the same, whatever befell him. His only joy lay in inspiring men to follow after the religion of the Gospel. And his efforts to this end were not in vain. Numbers both of men and women had he won to Christ, whose deathbeds showed how far they differed from the common run of Christians in these days. For you might have seen his disciples meet death with the greatest cheerfulness of spirit, singing a truly swanlike song at its approach and testifying by their utterances to a heart moved with a holy inspiration; while the rest, after performing the due rites and making the customary professions, would breathe their last—in assurance or doubt, as the case might be.

A witness of this fact was a distinguished physician of St. Omer named Ghisbert, a steady practicer of true religion and one who was present at the deathbeds of many persons of each party.

He had also won over some of the members of his own fraternity, though few by comparison, even as Christ could not do many mighty works among His own people. For men of his order are commonly best pleased with those who, by their teaching, bring most provisions to the kitchen, rather than with those who win most souls to Christ.

Averse from all vices as was that purest of souls, that temple truly dedicated to Christ, he recoiled most of all from licentiousness. The very atmosphere of such things was utterly repulsive to him: much less could he listen patiently to indecent language. Without ever indulging in bitter invectives, or disclosing anything gathered from private confessions, he would yet draw such a picture of virtue that every hearer tacitly recognized himself by the contrast. In giving counsel he showed singular prudence, integrity, and tact. While he would listen to private confessions—not, indeed, with any particular good will but following, in this respect also, the dictates of Christian charity—he openly expressed his dislike of oversolicitous and oft-repeated con-

fessions. To superstitious rites and ceremonies he attached
very little importance. He would eat of any kind of food
that there might be, though soberly and with giving of
thanks; and his dress was in no respect different from that
of others. It was his wont to take a journey occasionally for
the sake of his health at times when he felt overcharged
with bodily humors. So one day, while completing along
with his companion the allotted task of morning prayers,
feeling his stomach squeamish—by reason, perhaps, of his
having fasted the day before—he went into the nearest
house, and after taking something to eat there, resumed his
journey and was proceeding with his prayers. Thereupon
his companion thought that all would have to be begun
again from the beginning, seeing that he had taken food
before the prayers for Prime had been said. But he maintained with spirit that no fault had been committed, nay,
that God would rather be the gainer. "For while before,"
said he," we were slow and listless at our prayers, we shall
now utter spiritual songs to Him with ready minds; and
with such sacrifices—such as are offered by a cheerful giver
—God is well pleased."

At that time I was staying with Antonius à Bergis, the
abbot of St. Bertin.[5] Dinner was not served there till after-
noon; and as my stomach could not bear so long an abstinence (especially as it was Lent, and I was studying hard),
I was in the habit of staying my appetite before dinner with
a basin of warm soup in order to hold out till dinnertime.
On my asking Vitrier what he thought about the lawfulness
of my plan, he first gave a glance at the companion he then
had, who chanced to be a layman, for fear he should be at
all scandalized, and said: "Why, truly it would be a sin if
you did not act so, if for the sake of a morsel of food you

<hr/>

[5] Antonius à Bergis, or Antony of Bergen, was the brother of Henry of
Bergen, bishop of Cambrai, Erasmus' early patron. He had been forcibly
installed as abbot of the monastery of St. Bertin, in St. Omer, by his brother
in 1493.

were to interrupt those sacred studies of yours and injure your frail constitution."

When Pope Alexander, to gain ampler revenues, had made two jubilees instead of one, and the bishop of Tournai had bought as a speculation, for ready money, the privilege of granting dispensations from it, his commissaries began to use every effort that the bishop might not lose his investment but rather be the receiver of a handsome profit. Hereupon, such preachers as were acceptable to the people in their sermons were invited to be the first to play their part. Vitrier, observing that the money which had previously gone to the relief of the poor was now being put into the commissaries' boxes, did not approve of it, while yet not finding fault with what was offered by the pope. But this he did find fault with, namely, that people of scanty means should be defrauded of their accustomed support. He condemned also the foolish confidence of those who thought that by merely dropping a coin into the boxes they were freed from their sins. At length the commissaries offered him a hundred florins toward the building of the chapel in his convent, then in course of erection, on condition that if he were not willing to recommend the Papal indulgences, he would at least say nothing against them. Hereupon, as if prompted by some inspiration from above, he bade them begone with their simoniacal money. "Think you," he cried, "that I am one to keep back the truth of the Gospel for money? What if that does hinder your profits? I am bound to have a greater care for souls than for your gain."

For the moment they quailed, conscience-stricken, before the energy of this evangelic spirit. But in the interval, by early dawn next day, there was unexpectedly posted upon the church door a notice of excommunication against him— only to be torn down again by one of the townspeople, before any great number came to know about it. He, however, nothing daunted by these threats, went on teaching the people and sacrificing to Christ with the utmost composure of mind; nor did he show any fear of anathema, aimed at him for preaching Christ. Presently he was cited before the bishop of Boulogne. He obeyed his diocesan and, having no uneasiness about his own safety, went attended by only a single companion. But the townspeople, without his knowing it, had posted guards of horsemen on the road for fear that he might be waylaid and thrown into some den or other; for there is nothing on which the "accursed lust for gold" will not venture. When the bishop brought against him certain articles, gathered by his opponents from his sermons, he defended himself with spirit and satisfied his superior. Some time afterwards he was summoned afresh, and more articles were brought up against him. After replying to these in like manner, he asked why his accusers were not present to prefer their charges at their own risk as well as his. He had now come twice, he said, to show respect to him as his bishop, but he would not come a third time if similarly cited, for he had something better to occupy him at home. And so he was left to his own devices, either because his enemies had no pretext for injuring him or because they feared an uproar of the people. For, without his courting any such favour, his integrity had made all the most respectable men among them his devoted adherents.[6]

I know you will long have had the question on your lips, what the end of this man was. He offended not only the commissaries but also many of his own fraternity—not that they had any fault to find with his way of life, but because it was in fact too good to suit their interests. His heart was wholly set on winning souls. As to replenishing the larder, or erecting buildings, or inveigling young men of property— he was not so active for this as they could have desired. Not

[6] The comparison—and contrast—between this whole episode and Luther's indulgence controversy is most striking and is quite obviously stressed by Erasmus as a lesson for Jonas.

that he was inattentive, good man, to these duties either, provided that they tended in any way to relief of pressing want. But he did not, as so often happens, give them a disproportionate share of his attention. He had even gone so far as to estrange one supporter of the convent named Thynne.[7] This person was a courtier, and of decidedly courtierlike morals—a common invader of the marriage chamber, a promiscuous violator of wedded sanctities, one who had deserted his own wife, though a lady of high family and the mother of several children. By chance it fell out that she too went astray; on which he divorced the poor woman at the very first false step—he who had pardoned so many false steps in himself. She, sinking to lower and lower depths, came at last to the extremity of misfortune; for besides her degraded state, she fell victim to a loathsome disease. Vitrier tried every means to reconcile the husband and wife, but without success. The hardened reprobate was moved neither by respect for his wife's family, nor affection for their common children, nor by any twinges of conscience at having caused the mischief by his own frequent adulteries and neglect. And so Vitrier gave the man up as hopeless. Not long afterwards the latter sent, as he was accustomed to do, a ham or flitch of bacon to the convent. Now Vitrier, who was then filling the office of warden, had given orders to the porter to take nothing in without first calling him. Accordingly, on the arrival of the contribution, he was sent for. But on the servants presenting it with their master's compliments, he exclaimed: "Take back your load to the place you brought it from! We receive no devil's offerings here."

And so, though not ignorant that his life and teaching were a prolific nursery, so to speak, of Christian piety, yet,

---

[7] Allen (IV, 513.205n) points out that the word *thynnum* should not be understood as a proper name, as it is here, but that it means in this context "a fish caught in their net."

as he was not of equal service for provisioning the kitchen, they called upon him to resign the warden's office. This he did with as much good will as ever he did anything. In his stead there was appointed a man well known to me, whom they sent for from another neighborhood. Of what character he was, and what a contrast to his predecessor, I will not say; only that in my opinion he was one to whom no person of sense would have liked to entrust even his kitchen garden. Whether it was that he was thrust upon them by those who wished to get rid of him, or that they really thought him better suited for the office, I know not. But when still further, as the result of associating with Vitrier, there began to spring up a few other like-minded ones, whose absorbing passion was for serving the cause of Christianity and not for increasing the commissariat, they sent him away to a little convent of nuns at Courtrai. There, with character unchanged, still, so far as was allowed him, teaching, consoling, exhorting, he peacefully ended his days. He left behind him some treatises in French, in the way of extracts made from sacred writers; and these, I doubt not, are of a piece with the life and conversation of the author. Yet I hear that they are now condemned by some, who think it very dangerous for the people to read aught but the silly tales of histories or the dreams of monks.

There are many in whose breasts some sparks of his teaching still keep alive, and compared to these you would call other people rather Jews than Christians. Though held in such light esteem by his own community, I doubt not that, had this eminent man been allotted to the Apostle Paul for a colleague, he would have preferred him even to his own Barnabas or Timothy.

I have given you my jewel of a Vitrier, as he may truly be called, a man unknown to the world but famous and renowned in the kingdom of Christ. Now take his exact counterpart, Colet.

I had described each of them to the other, and they were both ardently desirous of seeing each other. In fact, Vitrier had crossed over to England with this object; and Colet related to me afterwards that he had had a visit from a Franciscan, with whose sensible and religious conversation he had been beyond measure delighted. But he added that he had brought with him a stoical companion of the same order, who seemed to take their Christian conversation amiss, and so cut short the interview.

It may indeed be that Colet deserves the greater praise of the two on this account, namely, that neither the smiles of fortune nor the impulse of a far different natural bent could divert him from the pursuit of a Gospel life. For he was the son of wealthy and distinguished parents; born, too, in London, where his father had twice filled the highest municipal office in his city, called by them the mayoralty. His mother, who still survives, is a most worthy woman. She bore her husband eleven sons and as many daughters; of whom John, as the eldest, would have been heir to the entire estate, according to the English law, even had the others been alive. But at the time when my acquaintance with him began, he was the sole survivor of the band. To these advantages of fortune was added that of a tall and graceful figure.

During his younger days in England he diligently mastered all the philosophy of the schools and gained the title expressive of a knowledge of the seven liberal arts. Of these arts there was not one in which he had not been industriously and successfully trained. For he had both eagerly devoured the works of Cicero and diligently searched into those of Plato and Plotinus, while there was no branch of mathematics that he left untouched.

After this, like a merchant seeking goodly wares, he visited France and then Italy. While there, he devoted himself entirely to the study of the sacred writers. He had

previously, however, roamed with great zest through literature of every kind, finding most pleasure in the early
writers, Dionysius, Origen, Cyprian, Ambrose, and Jerome.
I should add that among the old authors there was none to
whom he was more unfavorable than Augustine. At the
same time he did not omit to read Scotus and Thomas and
others of that stamp, if the occasion ever required it. He
was also carefully versed in treatises of civil and canon law.
In a word, there was no work containing either the chroni-
cles or enactments of our forefathers which he had not per-
used. The English nation has poets who have done among
their own countrymen what Dante and Petrarch have done
in Italy. And by the study of their writings he perfected his
style, preparing himself even at this date for preaching the
Gospel.

Soon after his return from Italy he left his father's
house, as he preferred to reside at Oxford, and there he
publicly and gratuitously expounded all St. Paul's Epistles.
It was at Oxford that my acquaintance with him began,
some kind providence having brought me at that time to the
same spot. He was then about thirty years old, some two or
three months younger than myself. Though he had neither
obtained nor sought for any degree in divinity, yet there
was no doctor there, either of divinity or law, no abbot or
other dignitary but came to hear him and brought his text-
books with him as well. The credit of this may have been
due to Colet's personal influence, or it may have been due to
their own good will in not being ashamed to learn, the old
from the young, doctors from one who was no doctor. However, the title of doctor was spontaneously offered him some
time later and accepted by him, though rather to oblige the
offerers than because he sought it.

From these sacred occupations he was called back to
London by the favor of Henry VII and made dean of St.
Paul's, so as to preside over the cathedral of that Apostle

whose epistles he loved so much. This takes precedence over all the deaneries in England, though there are others with richer incomes. Hereupon our good Colet, feeling his call to be for the work and not for the empty honor, restored the decayed discipline of the cathedral body and—what was a novelty there—commenced preaching at every festival in his cathedral, over and above the special sermons he had to deliver now at Court, now in various other places. In his own cathedral, moreover, he would not take isolated texts from the Gospels or Apostolic Epistles but would start with some connected subject and pursue it right to the end in a course of sermons: for example, St. Matthew's Gospel, the Creed, or the Lord's Prayer. He used to have a crowded congregation, including most of the leading men both of the city and the court.

The dean's table, which in former days had ministered to luxury under the guise of hospitality, he brought within the bonds of moderation. For having done without suppers entirely for some years before, he was thus free from company in the evening. Moreover, as he dined rather late, he had fewer guests on those occasions as well, and all the fewer because the repast, though neat, was frugal, and the sitting at table short, and lastly, the conversation such as to have no charms but for the good and learned. When grace had been said, a servant would read aloud in a clear, distinct voice a chapter from St. Paul's Epistles or the Proverbs of Solomon. He would then usually repeat some passage selected from the part read and draw a topic of conversation from it, inquiring of any scholars present, or even of intelligent laymen, what this or that expression meant. And he would so season the discourse that, though both serious and religious, it had nothing tedious or affected about it. Again, towards the end of the meal, when the requirements of nature, at any rate, if not of pleasure had been satisfied, he started some other topic; and thus bade farewell to his guests, refreshed in mind as well as in body and better men at leaving than they came, though with no overloaded stomachs. The pleasure he took in conversing with friends was extreme, and he would often prolong the talk till late at night. But still it was all either about literature or about Christ. If there was no agreeable person at hand to chat with—and it was not every sort that suited him—a servant would read aloud some passage from Holy Scripture. Occasionally he took me with him for company on a journey, and then nothing could be more pleasant than he was. But a book was ever his companion on the road, and his talk was always of Christ.

He could not endure any slovenliness, so much so as not to tolerate even an ungrammatical or illiterate mode of expression. All his household furniture, his service at table, his dress, his books he would have neat; as for splendor, he did not trouble himself. He used to wear only dark-colored robes, though priests and divines in England are usually robed in scarlet. His outer garment was always of woollen cloth, not lined; but if the cold required it, he would protect himself with an inner lining of fur.

All the revenue that came in from his preferments he left in his steward's hands, to be laid out in household expenses. His private fortune, a very large one, he would himself dispose of for charitable purposes. At his father's death he had inherited a large sum of money; and fearing lest, if he hoarded it up, it might breed some distemper of mind in him, he built with it in St. Paul's Churchyard a new school of splendid structure, dedicated to the Child Jesus. He attached to it also a handsome residence for the two masters to dwell in and assigned them a liberal stipend to teach free of charge, but on condition that the school should only admit a fixed number. The school was divided by him into four partitions. The one first entered contains those whom we may call the catechumens, none being admitted but such as can already both read and write. The second contains those under the surmaster's teaching, and the third those who are instructed by the high master. Each of these partitions is separated from the others by a curtain, drawn to or drawn aside at pleasure. Over the high master's chair is a beautifully wrought figure of the Child Jesus seated in the attitude of one teaching, and all the young flock as they enter and leave school salute it with a hymn. Over it is the countenance of God the Father, saying: HEAR YE HIM (an inscription added at my suggestion). At the far end is a chapel in which divine service may be held. The whole school has no bays or recesses, so much so that there is neither any dining room nor dormitory. Every boy has his own proper seat on regularly ascending tiers with gangways left between. Each class contains sixteen, and the head boy in each class has a stall somewhat higher than the rest. Boys of all kinds are not admitted promiscuously, but a selection is made according to natural capacity and ability.

A most farsighted man, Colet saw that a nation's chief hope lay in having the rising generation trained in good principles. But though the undertaking cost him a very large sum of money, he allowed no one to share it. Some person had left a legacy of a hundred pounds sterling toward the building. But when Colet perceived that on the strength of this outsiders were claiming some rights or other, he obtained his bishop's sanction to apply the sum toward providing sacred vestments for the cathedral. Over the revenues and the entire management of his school he placed neither priests, nor the bishop, nor the chapter (as they call it), nor noblemen, but some married citizens of established reputation. And when asked the reason, he said that, while there was nothing certain in human affairs, he yet found the least corruption in these.

This was a work that no one failed to approve. But many were surprised at his building a magnificent dwelling within

the precincts of the Carthusian monastery, not far from
what is called Richmond Palace. He said that he was preparing an abode for his old age, when he should be no
longer equal to his work or be enfeebled by sickness and so
compelled to retire from society. There he was minded to
philosophize with two or three chosen old friends, among
whom he was accustomed to reckon myself. But death forestalled him. For having been seized a few years before with
the sweating sickness (a disease that is the special scourge
of England), he was now for the third time attacked by it;
and though he recovered from it to some degree, an internal
disorder ensued from what the disease left behind it, of
which he died. One physician pronounced him dropsical.
Nothing fresh was discovered by the post-mortem examina-
tion except that the liver was found to have the extremities
of the lobes rough with tuftlike excrescences. He was buried
at the south side of the choir in his cathedral, in a modest
grave chosen by himself some years before for the purpose,
with the inscription placed over it: IOAN. COL.

Before I conclude, my friend Jonas, I will mention a few
particulars, first of his natural disposition, then of his peculiar opinions, and lastly of the stormy scenes in which his
sincere religion was put to the test. It was but a very small
portion of this religious spirit that he owed to nature. For
he was gifted with a temper singularly high and impatient
of affront; he was, as he himself confessed to me, naturally
prone to incontinence, luxuriousness, and indulgence in
sleep; overmuch disposed to jests and raillery; and he was
besides not wholly exempt from the taint of covetousness.
But these tendencies he combatted so successfully by philosophy and sacred studies, by watching, fasting, and prayer
that he led the whole course of his life free from the pollu-
tions of the world. As far as I could gather from my intimate acquaintance and conversations with him, he kept the
flower of chastity even unto death. His fortune he spent on

charitable uses. Against his high temper he contended with the help of reason, so as to brook admonition even from a servant. Incontinence, love of sleep, and luxuriousness he vanquished by a uniform abstinence from supper, by constant sobriety, by unwearied exertions in study, and by religious conversation. Yet if an occasion had ever presented itself either of conversing with ladies or being a guest at sumptuous repasts, you might have seen some traces of the old nature in him. And on that account he kept away, as a rule, from laymen's society, and especially from banquets. If forced at times to attend them, he would take me or some similar companion with him in order, by talking Latin, to avoid worldly conversation. Meanwhile he would partake sparingly of one dish only and be satisfied with a single draught or two of ale. He was abstemious in respect of wine, appreciating it if choice, but most temperate in the use of it. Thus keeping a constant watch upon himself, he carefully avoided everything by which he might cause anyone to stumble, not forgetting that the eyes of all were upon him.

I never saw a more highly gifted intellect. But though he felt a peculiar pleasure on this account in kindred intellects, he liked better to bend his mind to such things as fitted it for the immortality of the life to come. If at times he sought relaxation in sprightlier talk, he would still philosophize on every topic. He took a delight in the purity and simplicity of nature that is in children, a nature that Christ bids His disciples imitate, and he was wont to compare them to angels.

To complete, now, the second part of my promised account, his opinions differed widely from those commonly received. But in this matter he showed a remarkable discretion in adapting himself to others, so as to avoid giving offence to any persons or bringing any slur on his good name. For he knew well how unfair men's judgments are, how ready they are to believe evil, and how much easier a

thing it is for slanderous tongues to tarnish a man's good
name than for kind-spoken ones to repair it. Among friends
and scholars, however, he would express his sentiments with
the utmost freedom. As to the Scotists, for example, to
whom the common run of men ascribe a subtlety peculiarly
their own, he said that he considered them dull and stupid
and anything but intellectual. For it was the sign of a poor
and barren intellect, he would say, to be quibbling about the
words and opinions of others, carping first at one thing and
then at another, and analysing everything so minutely. Yet
for some reason he was even harder on Aquinas than on
Scotus. For when I once praised Aquinas to him as a writer
not to be despised among the moderns, since he appeared to
me to have studied both the scriptures and the early Fathers
—such being the impression I had formed from his *Catena
aurea*—and had also a certain unction in his writings, he
checked himself more than once from replying and did not
betray his dislike. But when in another conversation I was
reiterating the same opinions more strongly, he looked hard
at me, as if watching whether I were saying this in serious-
ness or in irony. And on perceiving that I was serious in
what I said, he broke out like one possessed: "Why do you
preach up that writer to me? For without a full share of
presumption, he never would have defined everything in
that rash and overweening manner; and without something
of a worldly spirit, he would not have so tainted the whole
doctrine of Christ with his profane philosophy." Struck
with his impetuous manner, I began a more careful study of
this author's writings, and, to be brief, my estimate of him
was undoubtedly diminished.[8]

Though no one approved of Christian devotion more
warmly than he, he had yet but very little liking for monasteries—undeserving of the name as many of them now are.
The gifts he bestowed upon them were either none or the

---

[8] Regarding Erasmus' view of Thomas Aquinas, see Renaudet, *Etudes
érasmiennes*, pp. 123–25. Also see Denys Gorce, op. cit., pp. 233 ff.

smallest possible, and he left them no share of his property even at his death. The reason was not that he disliked religious orders but that those who took them did not come up to their profession. It was in fact his own wish to disconnect himself entirely from the world, if he could only have found a fraternity anywhere really bound together for a Gospel life. And he had even commissioned me to seek for such a one when I was about to visit Italy, telling me that among the Italians he had discovered some monks of true wisdom and piety. Moreover, he did not consider what is popularly deemed religion to be really such, being as it often is mere poverty of intellect. He was accustomed also to praise certain Germans, among whom there even yet lingered, as he said, some traces of primitive religion. He was in the habit of declaring that he nowhere found more unblemished characters than among married people, on whom such restraints were laid by natural affection and family and household cares that they were withheld, as by so many barriers, from rushing into all kinds of wickedness. Though himself living in perfect chastity, yet of all in the list of offenders he was less hard on those—were they priests or even monks—whose only offence was incontinence. It was not that he failed to abhor the vice of unchastity but that he found such persons not nearly so bad, in comparison, as some others who thought no small things of themselves—though overweening, envious, slanderous, backbiters, hypocrites, empty-headed, ignorant, given up heart and soul to money-making and ambition—while their acknowledged infirmity rendered the former more humble and unassuming. Covetousness and pride, he would say, were more detestable in a priest than keeping a hundred concubines.

I would not have anyone strain these opinions to such a degree as to suppose incontinence in a priest or monk to be a slight offence, but only to infer from them that those of the other kind are still further removed from true religion. There was no class of persons to whom he was more opposed or for whom he had a greater abhorrence than those bishops who acted the part of wolves instead of shepherds, showing themselves off before the people with their guise of sanctity, their ceremonies, benedictions, and paltry indulgences, while at heart they were slaves to the world, that is, to ostentation and gain. He had a leaning to some opinions derived from Dionysius and the other early divines, though not to such a degree as to make him contravene in any points the decisions of the Church. Still, they made him less hard on such as disapproved of the universal adoration of images in churches, whether painted or of wood, or stone, or bronze, or silver; or again, on those who doubted whether a priest, openly and notoriously wicked, had any efficacy in the administration of the sacraments. Not that he in any way leaned to this error of theirs, but he was indignant against such as, by a life of open and unmixed depravity, gave occasion to surmises of this kind.

The colleges established in England at a great and imposing cost he used to say were a hindrance to profitable studies and merely centers of attraction for the lazy. And in like manner he did not attach much value to the public schools, on the ground that the race for professorships and fees spoilt everything and adulterated the purity of all branches of learning.

While strongly approving of auricular confession, saying that there was nothing from which he derived so much comfort and spiritual advantage, he yet as strongly condemned its too solicitous and frequent repetition. It is the custom in England for priests to celebrate the Holy Eucharist every day. But Colet was content to do so on Sundays and festivals, or at the most on some few days in addition, either because it kept him away from the sacred studies by which he used to prepare for preaching and from the necessary business of the cathedral, or because he found that he sacrificed with devouter feelings if he let an interval elapse. At the same time he was far from disapproving of the principles of those who liked to come every day to the Table of the Lord.

Himself a most learned man, he did not approve of that painful and laborious erudition which is made complete at all points, so to speak, by an acquaintance with all branches of learning and the perusal of every author. It was his constant remark that the natural soundness and simplicity of men's intellects were impaired by it, and they were rendered less healthy-minded and less fitted for Christian innocence and for pure and simple charity. He set a very high value on the Apostolic Epistles; but he had such a reverence for the wonderful majesty of Christ that the writings of the Apostles seemed to grow poor by the side of it. He had with great ability reduced almost all the sayings of Christ to triplets, intending to make a book of them. The rule that priests, even though busily occupied, must say long prayers right through every day, no matter whether at home or on a journey, was a thing that he greatly wondered at. As to the public service of the Church, he was quite of the opinion that that should be performed with proper dignity.

From numbers of the tenets most generally received in the public schools at the present day he widely dissented and would at times discuss them among his private friends. When with others, he would keep his opinions to himself for fear of coming to harm in two ways: that is to say, only making matters worse by his efforts, and sacrificing his own reputation. There was no book so heretical but he read it with attention. For from such, he said, he many a time received more benefit than from the books of those who so define everything as often to flatter their party leaders, and not seldom their own selves as well.

He could not endure that the faculty of speaking correctly should be sought from the trivial rules of grammarians. For he insisted that these were a hindrance to expressing oneself well and that result was obtained only by the study of the best authors. But he paid the penalty for this notion himself. For though eloquent both by nature and training, and though he had at his command a singularly copious flow of words while speaking, yet when writing, he would now and then trip on such points as critics are given to mark. And it was on this account, if I mistake not, that he refrained from writing books, though I wish he had not so refrained, for I should have been glad of the thoughts of such a man, no matter in what language expressed.

And now, that nothing may be thought wanting to the finished religious character of Colet, listen to the storms by which he was harassed. He had never been on good terms with his bishop, who was, to say nothing about his principles, a superstitious and impracticable Scotist, and thinking himself on that account something more than mortal.[9] I may say that, whilst I have known many of this school whom I should not like to call bad men, I have yet never to this day seen one who, in my opinion at least, could be termed a real and sincere Christian. Colet was no great favorite either with many of his own college, being too strict about canonical discipline; and these were every now and then complaining of being treated as monks, though in fact this college was formerly what in ancient deeds it is styled, the Eastern Monastery. However, when the animosity of the old bishop (who was, I should have said, full eighty years of age) was too virulent to be suppressed, he took as his coadjutors two other bishops, as wise and as acrimonious as himself, and began to give Colet trouble. His weapons were just what such persons resort to when plotting anyone's destruction, that is to say, he laid an information against him before the archbishop of Canterbury, specifying certain articles taken from his sermons. One was that he had

[9] The bishop referred to is Richard Fitzjames (c. 1440–1522), who had become bishop of London in 1506. Allen (IV, 518.365n) indicates his theological orientation was other than that described by Erasmus. He possessed manuscripts of Origen, Jerome, Augustine, Seneca, et al.

taught that images ought not to be worshiped. Another, that he had done away with the hospitality commended by St. Paul, seeing that in expounding the passage from the Gospel with its thrice repeated "feed my sheep," while he was in accordance with other expositors on the first two heads (feed by example of life; feed by the word of doctrine), he had disagreed with them on the third, saying that it was not meet that the Apostles, poor as they then were, should be bidden to feed their sheep in the way of any temporal support; and he had substituted some other interpretation in lieu of it. A third article was that having said in the pulpit that there were some who preached written sermons—the stiff and formal way of many in England—he had indirectly reflected on his bishop, who, from his old age, was in the habit of so doing. The archbishop, to whom Colet's high qualities were perfectly well known, undertook the protection of the innocent, and as Colet himself disdained any reply to these and still more frivolous charges, he became a protector instead of a judge. Still the old bishop's animosity was not allayed. He tried to excite the court, with the king at its head, against Colet, having now got hold of another weapon against him. This was that he had openly declared in a sermon "an unjust peace was to be preferred to the justest war,"[10] a war being at that very time in preparation against the French. A leading part in this play was being taken by two Franciscan friars, of whom one, a very firebrand of war, earned a miter while the other used to declaim like a Stentor in his sermons against poets—meaning Colet, who had not the least taste for poetry, though in other respects not unskilled in music. At this juncture the noble young king gave a conspicuous token of his kingly disposition, for he privately encouraged Colet to go on without restraint, and improve by his teach-

[10] Erasmus uses practically the same quotation, taken from Cicero, in the letter to Guy Morillon which appears in the Appendix.

ing the corrupt morals of the age, and not to withdraw his light from those dark times. He was not unaware, he said, of the motive that incited those bishops against him, nor unconscious of the benefits he had conferred on the English nation by his life and doctrine. He added, that he would put such a check on their attempts that others should clearly see that whoever assailed Colet would not go unpunished. On this, Colet expressed his gratitude for such kind feeling on the king's part but prayed leave to decline the offer. He would have no one, he said, worse off on his account: sooner than that, he would resign the office which he bore.

Some time afterwards, however, the faction had an occasion given them for hoping that now at last Colet might be crushed. An expedition was being got ready against the French, to start after Easter. On Good Friday, Colet preached a noble sermon before the king and his court on the victory of Christ, exhorting all Christians to war and conquer under the banner of Him their proper King.[11] For they, he said, who through hatred or ambition were fighting, the bad with the bad, and slaughtering one another by turns, were warring under the banner not of Christ but of the Devil. At the same time, he pointed out to them how hard a thing it is to die a Christian death, how few entered on a war unsullied by hatred or love of gain, how incompatible a thing it was that a man should have that brotherly love without which no one would see God and yet bury his sword in his brother's heart. Let them follow, he added, the example of Christ as their Prince, not that of a Julius Caesar or an Alexander.[12] Much more to the same effect he gave utterance to on that occasion, so that the king was in some

[11] This forthright sermon was preached before the court on Good Friday 1513. Erasmus' summary is all that remains of it. The only one of Colet's sermons that is extant is his Convocation Sermon of 1511 on the reformation of the Church, the English translation of which is reprinted in Nugent, op. cit., pp. 358–64.

[12] A clear and pointed reference by Colet to Pope Julius II, who had died just the month before (February 1513), and to his predecessor, Alexander VI.

apprehension lest the soldiers whom he was on the point of leading abroad should feel their courage gone through this discourse. On this, all the mischief-makers flocked together like birds setting upon an owl, in the hope that now at last the mind of the king might be exasperated against him. By the king's order Colet was sent for. He came and had luncheon in the Franciscan convent adjoining Greenwich Palace. When the king was apprised of his arrival, he went down into the convent garden, dismissing his attendants as Colet came out to meet him. As soon as they were alone, the courteous young prince bade him be covered and converse with him without ceremony, himself beginning in these terms: "To spare you any groundless alarm, Mr. Dean, we have not sent for you hither to disturb your sacred labors, which have our entire approval, but that we may unburden our conscience of some scruples, and with the help of your counsel may better discharge the duties of our office." (I will not, however, repeat the whole conversation, which lasted nearly an hour.) Meanwhile Bricot, who from a Franciscan friar had now become a bishop, was in high spirits in the palace, supposing Colet to be in danger; whereas the king and he were at one upon all points, save only that the king wished him to say at some other time, with clearer explanation, what he had already said with perfect truth, namely, that for Christians no war was a just one. And this was for the sake of the rough soldiers, who might put a different construction on his words from that which he had intended. Colet, as became his good sense and remarkable moderation of temper, not only set the king's mind at rest but even increased the favor in which he stood before. On returning to the palace, the king had a wine cup brought to him and pledged Colet in it before he would let him depart. Then embracing him most courteously and promising all that could be expected from the most gracious of sovereigns, he let him go. And as the throng of courtiers was now standing round, eager to hear the result of this conference, the king, in the hearing of all, said, "Let every man have his own doctor, and every one follow his liking; but this is the doctor for me." Thus they departed, like the baffled wolves in the adage, Bricot more than all; nor did anyone from that day forward venture to molest Colet.

I have now given you, Jonas, not finished portraits but outline sketches only—all that the scanty limits of a letter allowed—of two men of our age whom I consider to have been true and sincere Christians. It will be for you to select from each what you think most conducive to true religion. And if you ask which of the two I prefer, I deem them worthy of equal praise, considering that they were in circumstances so unlike. On the one hand, it was a great thing for Colet, in worldly circumstances such as his, to have steadily followed the call not of natural inclination but of Christ. On the other hand, the merit of Vitrier makes yet a fairer show in having attained, amid such conditions of life, to so much of the Gospel spirit as he displayed. It is as though a fish were to contract no marshy flavor, though ever living in a marsh. In Colet were some traits which showed him to be but man. In Vitrier I never saw anything that savored at all of human weakness. And if you take my word for it, Jonas, you will not hesitate to enroll these two in the calendar of saints though no pope should ever canonize them.

Happy spirits! to whom I owe much, aid by your prayers Erasmus, still struggling in the miseries of this life, that so I may rejoin your society, never to be parted from you more.

Adieu, Jonas! If I have done justice to your wishes, it is well. I have been far, I know, from doing justice to my subject.

Anderlecht, June 13, 1521

Autograph of Erasmus' letter to Guy Morillon, August 30, 1534.
Courtesy of the Pierpont Morgan Library.

Letter to Guy Morillon

AUGUST 30, 1534

Guy Morillon, to whom Erasmus addressed this letter, was a classical scholar who had become a secretary to Emperor (and King of Spain) Charles V. He had spent many years with Charles in Spain, and Erasmus addresses him there. The Peter Barbier referred to in the second paragraph had formerly been prominent at Charles's court and later became dean of Tournai. Erasmus accuses him of holding back money due him from a prebend at Courtrai. It was an old and tangled argument, and it would seem that Erasmus is hoping that Morillon might intervene on his behalf. The imprisonments mentioned in the final paragraph strike a pathetic note. John Vergara, a Spanish scholar, priest, and close friend of Erasmus, had been hailed before the Inquisition on charges of Lutheranism and was for a time imprisoned. The bishop of Rochester is, of course, John Fisher. Erasmus was in error regarding the imprisonment of John Stokesley, bishop of London.

The original autograph, reproduced here with permission, is in The Pierpont Morgan Library in New York City. It was purchased in 1955 from the Dutch Reformed Church, Austin Friars, London, to whom it was bequeathed, together with the letter collection of Abraham Ortelius, the sixteenth-century geographer, by Ortelius' nephew. The marginal notes are in the nephew's hand. The letter may be found in Allen, XI, 38–39.

Greetings! Since I have so great a friend as you in Spain, I am surprised that for several years now I have received no letters advising me on what is happening there. If you wish to know what Erasmus is doing, I am engaged in a severe and almost continual struggle with old age and with its companions arthritic feet and hands, indeed with arthritis in my whole system, and less frequently and severely with the stone. We are indebted to the graciousness of the emperor, who has preferred an unjust peace to a righteous war, that Germany has peace. The activity of the sects is still spreading and will break into flood at any time if it is not controlled. The Anabaptists—a race of men frenzied and devoted to death—have inundated lower Germany just as frogs and locusts once did Egypt. They have crept in under the cover of piety, but the outcome will be the seizure of the state; and how ominous it is that, although they teach absurdities, not to say impossibilities, and although they lay down harsh rules, the people nevertheless are drawn to that sect by some fatal attraction, or rather by the instigation of an evil demon.

Peter Barbier now clearly mocks me from afar. Having hedged behind marvelous excuses up till now, although he acknowledged that he wished to pay, he writes in his last letter that he has remitted payment as long as he can and that now he can do so no longer. I suspect that he has altered the agreement to his own advantage. Besides previous debts, he is now taking each year, and has for over five years, one hundred thirty French livres of my money. I have not yet decided how I must deal with this monstrous act. I am ashamed to brawl with a friend.

Vives writes that John Vergara, together with brother Tovar and several other learned men, is in prison. You know, I imagine, that the three most learned men in all of England are in jail: the bishop of Rochester, the bishop of London, and Thomas More, a dearer friend than any other I have ever had. Farewell.

ERASMUS OF ROTTERDAM, by my own hand.
Freiburg-im-Breisgau, August 30, 1534.

Bibliography

The following list is selective and contains (1) the main source collections of Erasmus' writings, (2) selected works of Erasmus in English translation, (3) recent and/or important books and articles about Erasmus and his times. It is intended both as a guide for further study and as a reference for the notes in this volume. Additional bibliographical information can be found in Vander Haeghen's *Bibliotheca Erasmiana* (Nieuwkoop, 1961; a reprint of the original Ghent edition of 1893). This work is particularly valuable for its listing of all editions of Erasmus' own works and editions. More recent bibliographies have been compiled by Jean-Claude Margolin: *Douze années de bibliographie érasmienne (1950–1961)* (Paris, 1963), and *Quatorze années de bibliographie érasmienne (1936–1949)* (Paris, 1969).

1. SOURCE COLLECTIONS

Erasmi Opera omnia. Ed. Johannes Clericus. 10 vols. Leyden, 1703–1706.
Erasmi Opera omnia. Amsterdam, 1969————. This new edition now in progress will run to approximately 30 volumes. 5 volumes have been published to mid-1975.
Opus epistolarum Des. Erasmi Roterodami. Edd. P. S. Allen, H. M. Allen, and H. W. Garrod. 12 vols. Oxford, 1906–1958.
Erasmi opuscula. Ed. W. K. Ferguson. The Hague, 1933.
The Poems of Desiderius Erasmus. Ed. C. Reedijk. Leyden, 1956.
Desiderius Erasmus Roterodamus: ausgewählte Werke. Ed. Hajo Holborn. Munich, 1933.
Douze lettres d'Erasme. Edd. Roland Crahay and Marie Delcourt. Paris, 1938.

2. ERASMUS IN ENGLISH

The correspondence and major writings of Erasmus are now being translated into English and published in a scholarly edition, *Collected Works of Erasmus*, by the University of Toronto Press. Approximately 40 volumes are planned, the first volume of which appeared in 1974: *The Correspondence of Erasmus. Letters 1 to 141 (1484 to 1500)*. Trans. R. A. B. Mynors and D. F. S. Thomson, annotated by Wallace K. Ferguson.

A. *Adagia* (1500 and after):

Phillips, Margaret Mann. *The "Adages" of Erasmus.* Cambridge, 1964. (A study with translations of many of the important adages.)

B. *Enchiridion militis christiani* (1501):

A Book called in Latin Enchiridion Militis Christiani and in English the Manual of the Christian Knight. London, 1905. (Edition of a 1533 English text attributed to William Tyndale.)

The Enchiridion. Trans. and ed. Ford Lewis Battles, in *Advocates of Reform from Wyclif to Erasmus,* ed. Matthew Spinka. (The Library of Christian Classics, Vol. xiv) London, 1953. Pp. 295–379. (Abridged.)
Erasmus, Handbook of the Militant Christian. Trans. John P. Dolan. Notre Dame, 1962. (Abridged.)
The Enchiridion of Erasmus. Trans. Raymond Himelick. Bloomington, 1963.

c. *Moriae encomium* (1509):

The Praise of Folly. Trans. John Wilson (1668), ed. Mrs. P. S. Allen. Oxford, 1913.
The Praise of Folly. Trans. Hoyt Hudson. Princeton, 1941.
The Praise of Folly. Trans. Leonard F. Dean. Chicago, 1946.
The Praise of Folly. Trans. Betty Radice, introd. A. H. T. Levi. Baltimore, 1971.

d. *De utraque verborum ac rerum copia* (1512):

On Copia of Words and Ideas. Trans. D. B. King and H. D. Rix. Milwaukee, 1963.

e. *Julius exclusus* (1513):

Julius exclusus. Trans. Paul Pascal. Bloomington, 1968.

f. *Institutio principis christiani* (1516):

The Education of a Christian Prince. Trans. Lester K. Born. New York, 1936.

g. *Querela pacis* (1517):

The Complaint of Peace. Introd. William J. Hirten. New York, 1946. (Facsimile edition of a 1559 English text.)

h. *De libero arbitrio* (1524):

Erasmus–Luther. *Discourse on Free Will.* Trans. and ed. Ernst F. Winter. New York, 1961.
Luther and Erasmus: Free Will and Salvation. Trans. and edd. E. Gordon Rupp *et al.* (The Library of Christian Classics, Vol. xvii) Philadelphia, 1969.

i. *Ciceronianus* (1528):

Ciceronianus. Trans. Izora Scott. New York, 1908.

j. *De sarcienda ecclesiae concordia* (1533):

Erasmus and the Seamless Coat of Jesus. Trans. Raymond Himelick. Lafayette, 1971.

k. *Familiarium colloquiorum formulae:*

The Colloquies. Trans. Nathan Bailey (1725), ed. E. Johnson. 3 vols. London, 1900.
The Colloquies of Erasmus. Trans. Craig R. Thompson. Chicago, 1965.

Inquisitio de fide, a Colloquy by Desiderius Erasmus Roterodamus. Ed. Craig R. Thompson. (Yale Studies in Religion, No. xv) New Haven, 1950; repr. 1975.

L. Writings on education:

Woodward, W. H. *Desiderius Erasmus concerning the Aim and Method of Education.* Cambridge, 1904; repr. 1964.

M. Letters:

The Epistles of Erasmus. Trans. and ed. Francis Morgan Nichols. 3 vols. London, 1901–1918; repr. 1962. (Letters through 1518.)
Erasmus and Cambridge: The Cambridge Letters of Erasmus. Trans. D. F. S. Thomson. Toronto, 1963.
Erasmus and Fisher. Their Correspondence, 1511–1524. Trans. Jean Rouschausse. Paris, 1968.
The Lives of Jehan Vitrier and John Colet. Trans. J. H. Lupton. London, 1883. (Translation of Erasmus' letter to Jodocus Jonas, June 13, 1521.)
"Selection from the Letters of Erasmus." Trans. Barbara Flower, appended to J. Huizinga, *Erasmus of Rotterdam.* New York, 1952.
Erasmus and His Age: Selected Letters of Desiderius Erasmus. Ed. Hans J. Hillerbrand, trans. Marcus A. Haworth, s.j. New York, 1970.

3. BOOKS AND ARTICLES ABOUT ERASMUS AND HIS TIMES

Several conferences were held to commemorate the five-hundredth anniversary of Erasmus' birth, and the papers delivered on these occasions have been published. Since these volumes afford a comprehensive introduction to recent Erasmus scholarship and contain a great variety of material, we list them at the head of this section.

Colloquium Erasmianum. Mons, 1968.
Scrinium Erasmianum. Ed. Joseph Coppens. 2 vols. Leyden, 1969.
Erasmus of Rotterdam. A Quincentennial Symposium. Ed. R. L. DeMolen. New York, 1971.
Colloquia Erasmiana Turonensia. Ed. J.-C. Margolin. 2 vols. Toronto, 1972.
Adams, R. P. *The Better Part of Valor.* Seattle, 1962.
Allen, P. S. *The Age of Erasmus.* Oxford, 1914.
———. *Erasmus: Lectures and Wayfaring Sketches.* Oxford, 1934.
Bainton, Roland H. *Erasmus of Christendom.* New York, 1969.
Bataillon, M. *Erasme et l'Espagne.* Paris, 1937.
Béné, Charles. *Erasme et Saint Augustin.* Geneva, 1969.
Bietenholz, P. G. *History and Biography in the Work of Erasmus of Rotterdam.* Geneva, 1966.
Bouyer, Louis. *Erasmus and His Times,* trans. F. X. Murphy. Westminster, 1959.
———. "Erasmus in Relation to the Medieval Biblical Tradition." *The Cambridge History of the Bible,* vol. II. Cambridge, 1969.
Chambers, R. W. *Thomas More.* London, 1938.
Chantraine, Georges. *"Mystère" et "Philosophie du Christ" selon Erasme.* Namur, 1971.

Coppens, Joseph. *Les Idées réformistes d'Erasme dans les préfaces aux paraphrases du Nouveau Testament.* Louvain, 1961.

Crahay, Roland. "Recherches sur le *Compendium Vitae* attribué à Erasme." *Humanisme et Renaissance,* 6 (1939), 7–19, 135–53.

Drummond, R. B. *Erasmus: His Life and Character.* 2 vols. London, 1873.

Etienne, Jacques. *Spiritualisme érasmien et théologiens louvanistes.* Louvain, 1956.

Febvre, Lucien. *Au Coeur religieux du XVIe siècle.* Paris, 1957.

———. *Le problème de l'incroyance au XVIe siècle. La religion de Rabelais.* Paris, 1942.

Froude, J. A. *Life and Letters of Erasmus.* New York, 1894.

Gerlo, Alois. *Erasme et ses portraitistes.* Brussels, 1950.

Gilmore, Myron. *Humanists and Jurists.* Cambridge, 1963.

Gorce, Denys. "La Patristique dans la réforme d'Erasme," *Festgabe Joseph Lortz.* Baden-Baden, 1958. i, 233–76.

Harbison, E. H. *The Christian Scholar in the Age of the Reformation.* New York, 1956.

Holeczek, Heinz. "Die Haltung des Erasmus zu Luther nach dem Scheitern seiner Vermittlungspolitik 1520/21." *Archive for Reformation History,* 64 (1973), 85–112.

Huizinga, J. *Erasmus of Rotterdam,* trans. F. Hopman. New York, 1952.

Hyma, Albert. *The Youth of Erasmus.* Ann Arbor, 1930.

Jarrott, C. A. L. "Erasmus' Biblical Humanism." *Studies in the Renaissance,* 17 (1970), 119–52.

Kaiser, Walter. *Praisers of Folly: Erasmus, Rabelais, Shakespeare.* Cambridge, 1963.

Kohls, E.-W. *Die Theologie des Erasmus.* Basel, 1966.

Kristeller, P. O. "Erasmus from an Italian Perspective." *Renaissance Quarterly,* 23 (1970), 1–14.

Lecler, Joseph. *Toleration and the Reformation,* trans. T. L. Westow. 2 vols. New York, 1960.

Lubac, Henri de. *Exégèse médiévale.* Second Part, ii. Paris, 1964.

Margolin, J.-C. *Erasme par lui-même.* Paris, 1965.

———. *Recherches érasmiennes.* Geneva, 1969.

Massaut, J.-P. "Humanisme et spiritualité chez Erasme." *Dictionnaire de spiritualité,* fasc. XLVI–XLVII, 1006–28.

McConica, J. K. *English Humanists and Reformation Politics under Henry VIII and Edward VI.* Oxford, 1965.

Mesnard, Pierre. *L'Essor de la philosophie politique au XVIe siècle.* Paris, 1936.

Oelrich, Karl Heinz. *Der späte Erasmus und die Reformation.* Münster, 1961.

Olin, John C. "Erasmus and St. Ignatius Loyola." *Luther, Erasmus, and the Reformation.* New York, 1969.

———. "The Pacifism of Erasmus." *Thought,* 50, No. 199 (December 1975).

O'Malley, John W. "Erasmus and Luther, Continuity and Discontinuity as Key to Their Conflict." *The Sixteenth Century Journal,* 5, No. 2 (October 1974), 47–65.

Payne, John P. *Erasmus: His Theology of the Sacraments.* Atlanta, 1970.

Phillips, Margaret Mann. *Erasmus and the Northern Renaissance.* London, 1949.

———. "Some Last Words of Erasmus." *Luther, Erasmus, and the Reformation.* New York, 1969.

Rabil, Albert, Jr. *Erasmus and the New Testament: The Mind of a Christian Humanist.* San Antonio, 1972.

Renaudet, A. *Erasme: sa pensée religieuse, d'après sa correspondance (1518–1521).* Paris, 1926.

———. *Etudes érasmiennes (1521–1529).* Paris, 1939.

———. *Erasme et l'Italie.* Geneva, 1954.

———. *Humanisme et Renaissance.* Geneva, 1958.

Reynolds, E. E. *Thomas More and Erasmus.* New York, 1965.

Rogers, Elizabeth Frances (ed.). *St. Thomas More: Selected Letters.* New Haven, 1961.

Schenk, Wilhelm. "The Erasmian Idea." *The Hibbert Journal,* 48 (1950), 257–65.

Seebohm, Frederic. *The Oxford Reformers.* London, 1869.

Smith, Preserved. *Erasmus.* New York, 1923.

Sowards, J. K. "The Two Lost Years of Erasmus," *Studies in the Renaissance,* 9 (1962), 161–86.

Spitz, Lewis W. *The Religious Renaissance of the German Humanists.* Cambridge, 1963.

Thompson, C. R. "Erasmus and Tudor England." *Actes du Congrès Erasme.* Amsterdam, 1971.

Tracy, James D. *Erasmus: The Growth of a Mind.* Geneva, 1972.

Vocht, Henry de. *Monumenta humanistica lovaniensia: Texts and Studies about Louvain Humanists of the First Half of the XVIth Century.* Louvain, 1934.

Index nominum